MACRO SYSTEMS IN THE SOCIAL ENVIRONMENT

Macro Systems in the Social Environment

Dennis D. Long
Xavier University

Marla C. Holle, MSW

F. E. Peacock Publishers, Inc.
Itasca, Illinois

Advisory Editor in Social Work

Donald Brieland
Jane Addams College of Social Work
University of Illinois at Chicago

Copyright © 1997
F. E. Peacock Publishers, Inc.
All rights reserved
Library of Congress Catalog Card No. 96-71591
ISBN 0-87581-409-3
Printed in the U.S.A.
Printing   10   9   8   7   6   5   4   3   2   1
Year   02   01   00   99   98   97

Contents

CHAPTER SIX

Young Adulthood   *141*

CHAPTER SEVEN

Middle Adulthood   *169*

CHAPTER EIGHT

Later Adulthood   *197*

Preface

Transitions in social work perspectives develop slowly. The traditional focus has been upon the interplay between the biological, psychological, and social aspects of human growth. This focus is rooted in the long-standing tradition in psychology of examining human maturation in individual terms.

The authors challenge the reader to a fresh and more inclusive view of human behavior and the social environment. We suggest a broader perspective that encompasses a macro-level understanding of the complexities of human development from infancy through later adulthood. This comprehensive framework offers expanded possibilities for intervention that will affect the social environment and empower the client to discover new problem-solving potential.

In this book, we have adopted social-psychological and sociological theories to assess the social environment—including social situations, conditions, and settings. In using a macro approach our goal has been to focus on the importance of organizations, communities, society, and global influences in social work assessment. By integrating social theory and current research with case examples, we challenge readers to shift their thinking away from individual pathology, family disequilibrium, or group conflict and to probe the larger social context.

Social work educators will find this outlook to be particularly useful as a complement to books and materials traditionally assigned in human behavior and social environment courses, as well as in macro-oriented practice courses. This book is designed specifically to address the concern of a growing number of social work educators relative to the need for greater infusion of macro-level content throughout the social work curriculum.

The use of well-known media figures and fictional characters to introduce various life-cycle topics is intended to provide a bridge for the student. In no way is our intent to trivialize social problems and issues. We hope instead that this approach will assist social work students in grappling with abstract principles as they relate to a diverse clientele.

Readers are encouraged to view the introduction to each chapter as an attempt to integrate social work content with everyday thinking. Our experience indicates that the challenge for many educators is to encourage students to go beyond the superficial and to critically analyze real-life persons, events, and occurrences. Our informal introductions are intended to promote insightful reading and understanding among students. We invite the reader to search for social meaning in newspapers, magazines, television and movies, sports events—indeed, in all aspects of life.

To assist students, noteworthy concepts and phrases are in bold type and defined. Theoretical orientations are provided early in each chapter to promote deductive reasoning. Theoretical considerations are revisited at the end of each chapter to encourage students to integrate chapter content and the case example with theory.

When considering the use of various social perspectives, readers need to keep two points in mind: first, most of the theories described in this book were not developed for social work practice; they are by definition more pure than applied. Theories are therefore offered to yield insights to social processes rather than to provide solutions.

Second, while only one theory was chosen to undergird each chapter, others could have been employed. Professors and students may enjoy debating the merits of using alternate macro theories in each chapter. Our design is not meant to imply that single theories should be used in social work assessment. Instead, the goal is to illustrate how numerous theories can be useful in assessing the social environment.

The names and locales of case examples provided throughout the book have been altered to protect confidentiality. Each example was developed with two objectives: consistency with chapter themes and portrayal of realistic situations. Cases reflect a blend of years of social work practice and selective creativity by the authors. Thus, any resemblance to real events is only coincidental.

— *Acknowledgments* —

We owe special appreciation to Richard Welna, Associate Publisher, and Ted Peacock, President of F.E. Peacock Publishers, Inc., for their encouragement, faith in our abilities, and support of our work. Additional thanks to Professor Donald Brieland, our consulting editor, John Beasley, our copyeditor, and Professor Diane Haslett, who has provided valuable insight and direction throughout the book.

We wish to express our gratitude also to Thomas M. Meenaghan, P. Neal Richey, Neil Heighberger, James Gaffney, Richard Sexton, Mary Trueheart Titzl, Jon Hoelter, and Michael Meier. We are in debt to these colleagues, mentors, and friends for their contributions to our intellectual and creative spirits.

Peg Hubbard, Kelly O'Donnell, and Tashawa Perrin have dedicated many hours of diligent work to the preparation and technical aspects of this book. We thank them for their expert assistance.

We remember our parents for their love and investment in our academic lives. A special thanks to our children—Noah, Jacob, Andrew, Todd, and Joan—for their understanding and support. We appreciate our spouses, Joan and Reg, who encouraged us to take on the challenge of coauthoring this book. Finally, we appreciate the interest that many of our friends have expressed in the unique professional and personal relationship that we enjoy as son-in-law and mother-in-law.

1

Macro Systems: Their Importance and Usefulness to the Social Worker

Reruns of the popular television show *M.A.S.H.* are familiar to most Americans. This highly successful series depicted the life of doctors and nurses in a mobile hospital unit during the Korean conflict. Surgeon Hawkeye Pierce's recurring complaint addressed the practice of patching up young, wounded soldiers in order to send them back into the war zone. "End the war, now!" was Hawkeye's frequent shout of frustration. The sound of approaching helicopters and the cry of "Wounded!" by the unit commander's aide, Radar O'Reilly, was a reminder that while health care professionals saved and mended bodies, the war and casualties continued.

Enabling soldiers to recover physically and mentally at a hospital, only to return to the battlefront, was but a microcosm of a much larger problem. If the war continued, then the

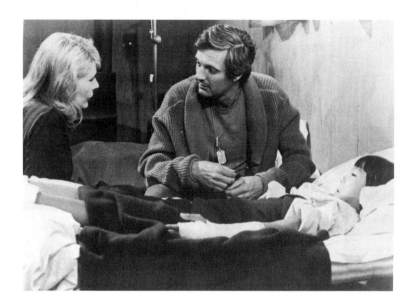

wounded would also continue to arrive in need of care. Tending to the sick and injured was not sufficient; addressing the larger (macro-level) issue of the war was necessary to bring an end to the human suffering.

Social workers often feel like Hawkeye. They are educated and trained to conceptualize human behavior in a holistic and systems-oriented context of the person in the social environment (Berger, Federico, and McBreen, 1991). The social environment includes "the cultural, economic, political, religious, indeed all aspects of everyday life" (Martin and O'Connor, 1989, p. 4).

While people served by social workers may not occupy military battlefields as do soldiers in *M.A.S.H.*, they often live in social battle zones of poverty and/or oppression. Clients frequently experience both social and economic catastrophe. Indeed, social workers often enter the profession to help eliminate specific social conditions that are the source of problems for clients. To avoid the feeling of helplessness in dealing with large-scale issues, social workers need to commit themselves to assessment and intervention with organizations, communities, society, and global issues. Social workers must shape their activities to goals aimed at eliminating poverty, discrimination, and social injustice.

However, the attack on social problems is a complex task. The large-scale battles confronting clients take various forms that encompass social systems on many levels.

Parsons (1951) portrays a **system** as a set of well-ordered, interrelated, and interdependent parts that share properties. Haynes and Holmes (1994) suggest that in social work these systems can be an individual, a family, a group, or a larger system—a community, state, nation, or world order.

"Social work typically refers to macro and micro as a way of distinguishing levels...big levels and small ones" (Garvin and Tropman, 1992, p. 90). Society, community, and organizations are part of **macro-level systems**. Individuals, family, and groups are **micro-level systems**. While each system is intrinsically complete, each relates to other systems or may constitute a subsystem of other larger social sets.

In social work education and practice, the relationships between large, macro systems and the client are major considerations (Siu, 1991). Rules and policies of organizations oppress various segments of our population. Segregation and poverty found throughout many of our communities are destructive forces. The lack of employment and absence of health insurance for millions of low-income families in the United States are societal-level problems with implications for nearly all Americans. Unfortunately, social service agencies often hire social workers to work exclusively with micro-level social systems, particularly individuals and families, with no personnel directed to macro-level system concerns.

This book is devoted to providing a broader, more comprehensive look at tactics and strategies for addressing the complex problems of our day. It describes specific life-cycle phases in relationship to macro-level system concerns and examples. The information provided here is intended to supplement and complement traditional readings in human behavior and the social environment that concentrate on micro-level systems involving casework, family therapy, and group work. Each of the following chapters highlights a selected social theory for analyzing macro-level issues. The chapters also provide case examples and illustrations stressing organizational, community, policy, and/or legislative concerns. These anecdotal materials are included to help social workers intervene with a client system during a specific developmental phase. Each "Time to Think!" section provides appropriate macro considerations for the generalist social worker to examine.

While social workers engaging in macro-level practice must also understand micro-level practice (Netting, Kettner, and McMurtry, 1993), the emphasis here is directed toward the macro level. Our goal is to have students "think big!" We encourage students to expand their thoughts about social work practice to national and international levels, while examining developmental issues of infants, preschool and elementary school children, adolescents, young adults, middle-aged adults, and older adults.

THEORY: ECOLOGICAL-SYSTEMS MODEL

A dominant theoretical approach for viewing human behavior in the social environment is the **ecological-systems model** (Germain, 1979). This model emphasizes the adaptive fit of human beings to elements of the environment, often referred to as the **person in environment**. Here, "person" refers to the client system. The client system can be an individual, family, group, or a social organization. The environment is all-inclusive, including both micro- and macro-level systems as well as resources required for sustenance. Common environmental elements include nuclear families or multigenerational clans, reference groups, the local community, a culture, a society or a nation, or an element of the international scene (Chetkow-Yanoov, 1992, pp. 7–8).

Using the ecological-systems model, the interface between human beings and their environment is conceptualized as bidirectional: Human beings affect the environment and the environment affects human beings. To look at either people or environments is insufficient. Instead, ecological theory focuses on the interaction between the two.

For a social worker, the challenge in using an ecological-systems orientation is to assess, simultaneously, the interrelated nature of the client, the client's situation, all relevant micro and macro social systems, and any other environmental factors. This is a **holistic approach** to social work assessment and intervention.

AN INSTITUTIONAL VIEW OF SOCIAL WELFARE

Social welfare is a necessary thread in the fabric of social structure, and society has a responsibility for the plight of its members. Social welfare should have a role of equal significance with other social institutions in our society, including the family, economics, political arenas, religion, and education.

Our fundamental premise is that people have intrinsic worth and are basically well intentioned, but they face routine and complex needs and problems of employment, food, shelter, and health care. In addition, since society helps create and perpetuate such social problems as unemployment, lack of affordable housing, and insufficient medical care, society has a responsibility to help remedy oppressive social conditions. Therefore, the social welfare institution is necessary not only for supplying goods and services to help clients cope with daily living, but for providing opportunities for clients throughout a society. In this **institutional or primary view of social welfare**, social services are seen as basic to the well-being of all people (Morales and Sheafor, 1989). Social services are one of society's first-line institutions for meeting human needs.

From our view, the macro-level content and activities suggested in subsequent chapters may appear to take a liberal or social-change slant. Much as Hawkeye perceived the war, the perspective presented here is geared more toward social reform than individual treatment. This view is not meant, however, to deny the need for individual responsibility and self-determination. On the contrary, the goal is to promote awareness of social issues while giving due respect to each client's struggle, responsibility, and choice.

Although social change comes gradually, widespread modifications are frequently achieved through organizations, communities, and societies, as well as globally—not only with individuals, families, and small groups. This suggests that poor people need not suffer continual oppression. Social conditions can improve when social workers form partnerships with economically disadvantaged persons. Together these partners can advocate at various levels for policies and programs that will improve their economic opportunities. Current economics, politics, and the marketplace have a major impact on these efforts.

Piven and Cloward's (1982) charge to educate and mobilize the traditionally alienated electorate to participate in politics and to vote is one example of how social workers and clients can actually work together to influence the larger environment. In reaction to President Reagan's attack on social welfare programs during the 1980s, Piven and Cloward declared the existence of a new class war in America. When it became evident that capitalists and corporate leaders of the '80s were moving to dismantle public relief and entitlement programs for the disadvantaged, Piven and Cloward began advocating for political reaction and protest for and by the unemployed, unemployable, and working poor who rely on social programs. Piven and Cloward publicly challenged social workers and social work students to actively engage the disadvantaged in political discourse and action aimed at thwarting President Reagan's attack on the social welfare state.

Piven and Cloward appeared on national television promoting voter registration for the poor. They implored social workers and social work students to consider innovative ways to educate clients about politics and voter responsibilities. As a result of their efforts, federal legislation has been passed to make voter registration easier.

Whether it was the result of outcries from social critics like Piven and Cloward or recognition of the need to advocate on behalf of the vulnerable, social workers became more politically active during the Reagan years (Ezell, 1993). Their involvement is evidenced by letters written to public officials, discussion of political issues, membership in politically active organizations, involvement in candidate elections, and attendance at political meetings.

Indeed, the problem of poverty has been traditionally important to social workers. The poor constitute an isolated group of people who are "systematically subjected to conditions that virtually eliminate all possibility of 'equal life chances'" (Ewalt, 1994, p. 149). Social workers have a rich tradition of practice with the poor as emphasized by Michael Harrington's *The Other America in the United States* (1963). When examining the behavior of clients who live in poverty, social workers must view their efforts in the context of our profession's long-standing commitment to eradicate economic oppression.

Social workers were at the front of President Johnson's War on Poverty during the 1960s. Education, training, and employment programs during this era benefited many citizens. During the Nixon administration, social workers debated the merits of a guaranteed annual income for all Americans, even though such legislation was never enacted. Through the decades, irrespective of the president or political party in power, social work has championed the cause of the less fortunate.

Welfare reform legislation in 1996 was a concern to many social workers as it threatened to harm children and throw thousands into poverty. The 1996 legislation:

1. Gives states even greater control over welfare
2. Limits lifetime benefits per family

3. Requires adults to work after two years
4. Limits benefits to U.S. citizens and legal immigrants
5. Reduces federal spending on welfare by approximately $55 billion over six years

APPROPRIATE VALUE ORIENTATION

Social workers must guard against a naive perception of life. As the rich get richer, the efforts to secure scarce resources for the poor become increasingly competitive and complex. Indeed, low-income families are likely to report specific problem areas pertaining to needs for safe neighborhoods, child support, steady income, housing, jobs, and schools (Proctor, Vosler, and Sirles, 1993). So, to view a problem for assessment and intervention without considering factors such as economic status, race, neighborhood, and other environmental conditions is to fail to appreciate the complexities of the problem.

The value orientation for social workers is rooted in the National Association of Social Workers' (NASW) recently revised (1996) Code of Ethics, which emphasizes a respect for the unique life experiences of individuals and groups with a commitment to client self-determination. However, for social workers to profess to know the true feelings of any client in need would be a fallacy. The gut-level of oppression or need is unique for each person and client. As a result, the goal is to respond nonjudgmentally and to attempt to grasp the situation of each client.

To emphasize this point, a colleague had students perform a simple exercise. He asked each student to hold his or her breath as long as possible. Then, in the complete silence of the classroom, the professor instructed students to breathe as needed. Next, the students described what they thought about while holding their breath and how they felt. Did any two students experience exactly the same sensation? How important did that next breath of air become? Did the students think of anything other than that next breath?

This exercise focuses on the desperate nature of human problems. In their struggle to attain the basics of life, clients typically focus on relieving the pain resulting from their immediate needs. When clients have life-threatening needs is it helpful to raise macro-level issues? This chapter will show that both micro- and macro-level issues are appropriate concerns for the helping process.

CASE EXAMPLE

Betty Johnson is a 21-year-old senior and social work major in a field placement at **Friendship House**, a shelter for homeless women and children in northern Kentucky. Betty grew up in a middle-class white family from the suburbs of Louisville. Her parents expressed concern about her career choice of social work. Her father's reluctance focused on low earnings, her mother's on safety. But Betty convinced them that social work was her calling.

Betty's first client was Dorothy McCoy, an 18-year-old single parent with two daughters, ages three and two. This Appalachian mother and her children were homeless and without an income. Her husband, an alcoholic, had left the state to seek a new start. Unable to pay her rent, Dorothy lost her apartment in Oldtown, Kentucky, and was searching for housing. She was but one person in the growing numbers of homeless women with minor children (Mills and Ota, 1989).

As Dorothy seated herself at Betty's desk, her first words to the social worker were, "How old are you and how many kids do you have?" Somewhat startled by this opening question, Betty disclosed that she was 21, unmarried, and had no children. Two worlds began to collide!

Disbelieving, Dorothy asked, "Where do you live?" and continued to confront the worker. "Everybody I know has been married at least once or has children by your age.... I may not have much, but I have been around and I know what is happening!... How are you going to help me?"

Betty Johnson is learning about a world she has not experienced. While Oldtown, Kentucky, has made great strides in recent years with regard to urban development, it is known by many in the area as a tense and dangerous community. Sections of Oldtown are characterized by nude dancing establishments, bars, poor housing, and poverty. By contrast, other areas of Oldtown, overlooking the Ohio River, are characterized by expensive homes and successful businesses. Dorothy McCoy has lived her entire life in the Oldtown slums. Across the bridge the city of Cincinnati seems to promise there is more to life than poverty.

For the past five years, Dorothy and her children survived on the small amount of money left after her husband's alcoholic needs were met. She had friends in Oldtown, most of whom lived in similar circumstances. Her only possessions—three suitcases full of clothes and a few furniture items—were stored with one of her friends. Dorothy's goal was to find housing and work as soon as possible.

Only minimum-wage service jobs in fast-food restaurants or room cleaning for cut-rate motels were available in Oldtown for unskilled persons such as Dorothy. These settings provided no guarantee of a 40-hour work week or regular working hours and no health care benefits for herself and two young children. Child care presented an additional concern and expense. Public buses were Dorothy's only option for transportation to her job and child care. Locating housing, though her most pressing need, was only one of a complex pattern of concerns.

Meanwhile, Betty was unsure how to respond to Dorothy's confrontational remarks. While Betty had been sensitized to cultural differences during her student field placement, she was not prepared for Dorothy's hostility.

As Betty began to build a relationship with Dorothy in order to assess the situation, many problems surfaced. Dorothy had lived a very different lifestyle than Betty. Her expectations concerning the future, employment, and housing also differed from Betty's understanding of life goals. Betty sensed that Dorothy's primary need was for a safe environment. Betty also began to realize that Dorothy was typical of women served at

Friendship House and that many women in America face similar circumstances.

TIME TO THINK!

What macro-level issues come to light with this case? As a social worker, what kind of macro-level activities should Betty consider in order to promote structural kinds of changes that might benefit clients like Dorothy? How does this client's neighborhood and social setting dictate avenues the worker can explore? How can Betty begin to establish a partnership with Dorothy to address macro-level concerns?

SCANNING MACRO SYSTEMS

Let's scan different social-system levels and condition ourselves to think about the relevance of larger social systems to this case. Given the information as we know it, what are some issues at the organizational, community, society, or global levels that Betty should consider? Beyond personality traits and family circumstances, macro aspects of the social environment must be assessed.

Organizational Level

When examining the client-in-environment situation, social workers must consider the full range of organizations that may assist the client. An obvious beginning would be the services offered by the social worker's agency. In this case, Friendship House can provide short-term emergency housing, food, clothing, and financial counseling to Dorothy. But understanding the organization involves more than a description of available programs. To ascertain the availability of resources to the client, the social worker must be familiar with the organizational structure and power bases, formal and informal, that are unique to the social service agency.

As an example, the response of administrators of social work agencies may vary by case as they consider which scarce resources should be allocated to which clients. This protects the organization from overcommitting funds on a purely categorical basis—that is, where benefit allotments are predetermined according to classification of need. Flexibility in distributing goods and services allows agencies to use discretion while maintaining reserves for emergencies.

In a similar fashion, Betty will need to be cognizant of the social structure and politics of interacting with other social service agencies in northern Kentucky. As an example, it is not unusual for social workers to "call in favors" from other social workers with whom they have cooperated in the past. It will be to Dorothy's benefit that Betty is known and respected at social service agencies that frequently interact with social workers at Friendship House. Betty needs to be aware of the dynamics of informal networking and its appropriate use in addressing clients' needs.

As the social worker continues to intervene, she may find out about apartment rental companies in the area and the availability of subsidized housing. DiNitto (1995) indicates that 64 percent of families receiving Aid to Families with Dependent Children (AFDC) rent private housing but 23 percent reside in public housing. Does Dorothy belong to a church that participates in a housing program or is there an organization that might help Dorothy find temporary housing?

What companies in the area would be willing to hire Dorothy? Are there day care facilities or other child care resources available? Contacts and knowledge of local employers and day care options are critical to improving Dorothy's situation.

An array of other social service organizations should also be considered. What resources are available at the local Salvation Army, food and clothing banks, public housing authority, women's centers, or the Cabinet of Human Resources? Can contact people at these organizations provide information and new ideas that will assist Dorothy?

Organizations, much like individuals, operate via social exchange (Blau, 1964). To improve Dorothy McCoy's situation, Betty Johnson will use her knowledge of local employers and day care options. It benefits the client for the social worker to nurture relationships with people in various community organizations. While social workers often adequately network with people at other social service agencies and organizations, a greater challenge is to build contacts with area businesses and other for-profit organizations.

An example of successful networking with business is a Cincinnati-based convenience store's corporate sponsorship of Friendship House. Beyond the provision of food and hygiene products, this corporation donates time and expertise in connection with fund-raising, public relations, and special projects at this neighborhood agency. This company has also created an employment program for residents at Friendship House in their search for jobs.

Community Level

The community in which one resides often restricts what one can or cannot do in life. The availability of resources within the community can be an empowering or limiting factor for people.

What do we know about Dorothy's neighborhood? What stereotypes are associated with economically disadvantaged Appalachians living in urban areas in northern Kentucky? Does Dorothy have available a neighborhood/community-based support system? How do friends and neighbors influence her behavior? How can such a support system benefit Dorothy and her children?

Betty will want to become involved in local northern Kentucky housing coalitions like Housing Incorporated, a nonprofit organization. Its mission is to provide decent, affordable housing opportunities and to support families and individuals with very low income. As a result of this involvement, Betty will be more informed about community resources available to Dorothy and other clients facing similar situations.

Each community, like every individual, has distinctive differences. Communities vary in size, affluence, and commitment to the less fortunate. As a practicing social worker, Betty may never be fully accepted by Dorothy's local community, but she can gain stature and respect within the neighborhood and acquire the information about Dorothy's community that she needs in order to be an effective practitioner.

To gain acceptance, it is important for Betty to be perceived as a sensitive, professional social worker in the communities in which she practices. If people in a community are convinced that Betty is knowledgeable and cares about their welfare, she has crossed a major social hurdle. Betty's positive participation in community functions (the downtown renovation project, the fine arts drive, and the homeless coalition) will open doors for her in assessing the impact of the community on Dorothy's presenting situation.

In her role as a social worker, Betty must be a student of this new culture. To help Dorothy make sense of the complex pieces of her life, Betty needs an accurate sense of the community and its role in her client's life. At this point, Dorothy may be skeptical of Betty and unsure that she understands her situation. Building a base of trust and respect with Dorothy and in the community will be among Betty's first goals.

Societal Level

In Mead's classic work *Mind, Self, and Society* (1934) he describes the relationship between one's self and the society in which one lives. A basic tenet of Mead's theory is that who we are is influenced by how others view us.

Given this premise, how does society view people like Dorothy? For example, popular media conservatives, such as Rush Limbaugh, often portray needy persons as irresponsible and lazy—freeloaders looking for handouts! And a powerful segment of our population seeks to curtail or eliminate programs and services for the poor and needy (Piven and Cloward, 1982). The growing clamor demands that those who require help should "pull themselves up by their own bootstraps." Many citizens expect people like Dorothy to be self-sufficient and forgo assistance from the government and social service agencies.

Where does such an ideology leave Dorothy? Is emergency assistance more acceptable to the general population than institutionalized welfare programs? What are Dorothy's feelings about asking for aid?

Americans tend to think of the homeless in the United States as a "faceless group" (Hartman, 1989, p. 483). Employing such a view enables people to distance themselves from the problem. With the continuing misconception that homeless people are usually drunkards or irresponsible misfits, the societal crisis in housing is often seen in the United States as the private troubles of those who deserve their lot in life.

A client does not live in a vacuum. Dorothy and her children are not alone in their domestic plight. Many other American families face homelessness due to divorce, mental illness, physical limitations, substance abuse, and abandonment. But this does not negate the stigma that will confront Dorothy McCoy and challenge Betty Johnson.

International Level

International issues directly affect the problems presented by Dorothy to Betty. Clients are an integral part of their environment, and the environment directly affects the person and the problem. Northern Kentucky is only a microcosm of the "global village" in which we all live.

In the greater Cincinnati area companies like Procter & Gamble, Kroger's, and Delta Airlines have home or regional offices. These businesses have strong international components and serve as major employers and influences upon communities in northern Kentucky.

The Greater Cincinnati and Northern Kentucky Airport is located in northern Kentucky, only minutes from Dorothy's home. Construction projects from this airport are expected to contribute over $2 billion to the local economy in the next 15 years. In terms of tourism and related spending, the airport will help generate 160,000 jobs to the local area and over $11 billion in business by the year 2001 (Airport Connections, 1995).

On the other hand, if Procter & Gamble were to leave the Cincinnati area, people in that city and northern Kentucky would be economically devastated. Betty needs to be alert to both national and international economic influences that impact clients.

Several years ago Newport (Kentucky) Steel Company faced grave economic hardship due to the downturn of the international climate in the steel industry. Social workers should not underestimate the effect of changes and fluctuations in businesses that are key to the local economy. When people are displaced from employment, make salary concessions at work, or fear for their jobs, stress is created for individuals and families.

Conversely, when international enterprises move into communities, creating a flurry of jobs and bringing new monies into the area, booms often occur. In Georgetown, Kentucky, one hour away from Oldtown, Toyota opened a factory that provided hundreds of jobs, skilled and unskilled. In the age of multinational corporations and global economic inequalities (Braun, 1991), social workers must be sensitive to national and international conditions that have direct or indirect consequences for clients.

APPLYING A SOCIAL WORK FRAMEWORK: ECOLOGICAL SYSTEMS

Each chapter in this book uses a different social theory to analyze chapter content and case examples. In this chapter, a general ecological-systems approach has been introduced as an important perspective when examining human behavior in the social environment. An ecological-systems approach highlights the significance of relationships between clients and the various systems with which they interact on a daily basis. Schools, workplaces, churches, neighborhoods, social work agencies, and even countries are integral to the functioning of individuals, families, and groups of people. Many of these elements will be addressed in "Time to Think!" sections.

Effective assessment and intervention from a social work perspective requires a keen awareness of the dynamic and changing social environment in which clients live. As an example, social workers in the '90s will be at the forefront of managed health and mental health care and the emergence of multidisciplinary intervention teams in America. **Managed health care** is a term used to describe the method by which insurance companies and funding sources implement policies and programs directed at containing costs of medical services, while attempting to maintain effective intervention. Managed health care often involves the establishment of **interdisciplinary group practices** of professional social workers, psychologists, counselors, nurses, psychiatrists, and physicians who join forces to create a corporate entity aimed at addressing client needs in an efficient and cost-effective manner.

The era of private practice may be nearing an end. Fueled by the health care reform movement and federal changes in Medicaid funding, interdisciplinary group practices have begun to replace the individual practitioner/physician model in the United States.

While overlap exists among various helping professionals relative to theoretical orientations and approaches for intervention, each profession is characterized by a distinct and special focus. For social workers, utilizing macro-level systems analysis during assessment and problem solving is essential. The inclusion of larger social systems is a unique aspect of professional social work to be shared with other professionals.

At Xavier University in Cincinnati, Ohio, the Social Work Program offers a team-taught Human Life Cycle II course examining a broad range of information from adolescence through older age. A social worker and a psychologist work together to impart substantive content and theories related to human growth and development.

The instructors in this course use contrasting styles and approaches. During class, they each stress their discipline's views of human behavior but are sensitive to the other's professional training and experience. In the classroom, with students as active participants, discussions and debates reflect the multidisciplinary workplace in which many social workers practice.

In such a contemporary practice environment, an explicit goal for each professional is to work for the greatest benefit of each client. Group practices are typically organized with a division of labor that matches client problems to the appropriate provider(s). Toward this end, social workers must be articulate advocates of a social work perspective in each multidisciplinary endeavor.

Tower (1994) suggests certain orientations for helping that are unique to social workers. One such orientation is that of a "consumer-centered" approach in intervention. When social workers view clients as consumers they must also respect them as people who are actively involved, self-determined, and seeking control of their lives.

In an interdisciplinary intervention climate, one challenge for social workers is to promote among various team members a clear and unequivocal understanding of the active role of clients in assessing their problems. As social workers, we enable our colleagues to view presenting problems as more than personal or family conflicts. It is our responsibility to interpret for others the potential benefits of macro-scale social change and political action for clients (Feld, 1991).

With respect to the case example involving Dorothy McCoy, the social worker constructs a complete picture highlighting the interface between client and environment. Dorothy's neighborhood and the subculture in Oldtown, Kentucky, are important elements for consideration. Opportunities for employment, day care, and affordable housing are critical components for women who are homeless with children. The future for Dorothy and her children is contingent upon many macro- and micro-level system factors as well as upon Dorothy's motivation and will to succeed. As a social worker, Betty Johnson will also need to be actively involved in any social changes or policy considerations that might relate to her client's case. Welfare reform initiatives, changes in Medicaid policies, housing legislation, and modifications in child support assistance programs are areas of potential importance to young mothers.

Dorothy McCoy and her children also have physical and mental health needs. The restructuring of services under managed care has broad implications for her and many other clients. Variables such as the number of health and mental health providers, accessibility and availability of providers, and the professional composition of provider groups will influence assessment and treatment decisions. Environment and resource issues are focal points for social workers involved in the managed care movement.

To address the client's immediate needs, Betty helped Dorothy to secure subsidized housing and AFDC. Dorothy's desire, however, was to become fully employed and self-sufficient. With encouragement and support from Betty, Dorothy examined various job opportunities in the community. By networking with local businesses, Betty facilitated several interviews for Dorothy with promising employers. Dorothy and Betty also explored various day care and housing options. With each day, Dorothy and Betty became more knowledgeable about the available resources in Oldtown, northern Kentucky, and the Cincinnati area.

SUGGESTED ACTIVITIES

1. Some organizations offer programs and retreats for experiencing various subcultures and lifestyles. Consider taking an "urban plunge" or spending some time in an unfamiliar subculture, such as an Appalachian community. The ability to assess values, norms, and strengths in less-familiar areas is a valuable asset for social workers.

2. Many social work students volunteer time and energy to social causes prior to entering field placement. Homeless shelters and centers serving women are two examples of organizations that can sensitize students to the plight of special population groups. Identify social problems or population groups in need of student volunteers.

3. Share your insights with classmates concerning socioeconomic crises that exist in your hometown or a nearby community. Consider social and ethnic composition, economic promise, employment opportunities, and housing concerns. Identify local, state, or national influences on the disadvantaged in your geographical area.

────────────────── **REFERENCES** ──────────────────

Airport Connections (1995). Flying High: Airport Impact to Top $11 Billion a Year. Cincinnati/Northern Kentucky International Airport Communications Department, Cincinnati, OH.

Berger, R., Federico, R., & McBreen, J. (1991). *Human Behavior: A Perspective for the Helping Professions.* New York: Longman.

Blau, P. (1964). *Exchange and Power in Social Life.* New York: John Wiley.

Braun D. (1991). *The Rich Get Richer.* Chicago: Nelson-Hall.

Chetkow-Yanoov, B. (1992). *Social Work Practice: A Systems Approach.* New York: The Hawthorne Press.

DiNitto, D. (1995). *Social Welfare: Politics and Public Policy.* Boston: Allyn and Bacon.

Ewalt, P. (1994). Poverty Matters. *Social Work*, 39(2), 149-151.

Ezell, M. (1993). The Political Activity of Social Workers: A Post-Reagan Update. *Journal of Sociology and Social Welfare*, 10(4), 81-97.

Feld, K. (1991). Advocacy Heals. *Headlines*, 2, 11-16.

Garvin, C., & Tropman, J. (1992). *Social Work in Contemporary Society.* Englewood Cliffs, NJ: Prentice-Hall.

Germain, C. (1979). *Social Work Practice: People and Environments.* New York: Columbia University Press.

Harrington, M. (1963). *The Other America in the United States.* Baltimore: Penguin Books.

Hartman, A. (1989). Homelessness: Public Issue and Private Trouble. *Social Work*, 34(6), 483-484.

Haynes, K., & Holmes, K. (1994). *Invitation to Social Work.* New York: Longman.

Martin, P., & O'Connor, G. (1989). *The Social Environment: Open System Applications.* New York: Longman.

Mead, G. (1934). *Mind, Self, and Society.* New York: Doubleday.

Mills, C., & Ota, H. (1989). Homeless Children with Minor Children in the Detroit Metropolitan Area. *Social Work*, 34(6), 483-489.

Morales, A., & Sheafor, B. (1989). *Social Work: A Profession of Many Faces.* Boston: Allyn and Bacon.

Netting, F., Kettner, P., & McMurtry, S. (1993). *Social Work Macro Practice*. New York: Longman.

Parsons, T. (1951). *The Social System*. New York: Free Press.

Piven, F., & Cloward, R. (1982). *The New Class War: Reagan's Attack on the Welfare State and Its Consequences*. New York: Pantheon Books.

Proctor, E., Vosler, N., & Sirles, E. (1993). The Social-Environmental Context of Child Clients: An Empirical Exploration. *Social Work*, 38(3), 256-262.

Siu, S. (1991). Providing Opportunities for Macro Practice in Direct Service Agencies: One Undergraduate Program's Experience. *Arete*, 16(2), 146-151.

Tower, K. (1994). Consumer-Centered Social Work Practice: Restoring Client Self-determination. *Social Work*, 39(2), 191-196.

2

Infancy

Eric Clapton's famous ballad, "Tears in Heaven," an ode to his deceased son, expresses a grieving father's pain and sorrow. Four-year-old Conor Clapton died as the result of an accidental fall from an open hotel window in 1991. In the lyrics, Clapton addresses his lost son as he asks, "Would you know my name, if you saw me in heaven?"

While Eric Clapton is known in the entertainment world as a survivor of drug addiction, alcoholism, and the loss of close musical colleagues Jimi Hendrix and Stevie Ray Vaughan, he will probably best be remembered for "Tears in Heaven," "His Saddest Song" (*Newsweek*, 1992). This song is unique because Conor was Eric Clapton's own son and the pain he expresses in these lyrics was vivid and personal to him.

The high probability of death for young children during the first years of life is a chilling social fact—a dreadful topic frequently avoided in everyday conversation. It seems unfair when the joy and excitement of human birth is clouded by the risk of infant death. Research indicates that thousands of infants die each year because of preventable conditions including poverty, poor health care, and abuse (Combs-Orme, Risley-Curtiss, and Taylor, 1993).

From a global perspective, it might be assumed that, with its medical resources, the United States fares well with respect to **infant mortality**, the deaths of infants under one year of age (measured per 1,000 live births). Yet, internationally the United States ranks 24th in infant mortality and 19th in **post-neonatal mortality**, deaths occurring during the last 11 months of the first year of life (National Center for Health Statistics, 1993). Within the United States, socioeconomic differences among various groups contribute directly to disturbing differentials in infant mortality rates. The most glaring factor in this inequality is racial.

In the United States, African-American infants die at a rate nearly twice the white infant death rate (Zopf, 1992, p. 91). This differential is directly related to the availability of proper prenatal and postnatal care. While Americans take great pride in being a country of high technology, it is evident that all people do not have equal access to life-saving medical technology in our society. As an example, Andrejevic (1995) reports that in 1994 "18.4 of every 1,000 babies born to black women in Michigan died within 12 months...down from 18.8 per 1,000 in 1993.... For whites in the state, the 1994 death rate was 6.5 per 1,000, down from 7.1 percent the year before."

For many children in the United States, the tragic reality is that health care and medical services remain either inadequate or unavailable. As a result, infants born to economically disadvantaged parents are at a higher risk of life-threatening illnesses, disabling conditions, and death. Social work practice verifies this trend as social workers deal with premature and failure-to-thrive babies, sudden infant death syndrome (SIDS), child abuse, and infants who dwell in accident-prone environments. Social workers know that proper nutrition, medical care, and nurturing living conditions are fundamental to the survival and healthy development of children.

This chapter began with a tragic, true story. However, one might question the merits of emphasizing infant mortality over the miracle of the beginning of life. As we begin to examine human life-cycle phases, our goal is to use macro perspectives that extend beyond personal tragedy and move toward more comprehensive solving of social problems.

The grief of losing a child, as experienced by Eric Clapton, is far from an uncommon event in the United States. However, less prestigious families seldom have the opportunity to tell about a child's death in major newspapers or magazines. While many Americans shared the sadness at the accidental loss of Conor Clapton, few Americans hear of the thousands of children who die each year in the United States as a result of inadequate sustenance and lack of health care and medical services. How many children could be spared each year if health and medical care existed for all in America?

THEORY: SOCIAL DISORGANIZATION

Problematic behavior can be conceptualized in different ways. The tendency to assign responsibility to individuals for problems is frequently referred to as **personal blame**. When social phenomena and social change are viewed as producing unacceptable behavior, we engage in **system blame** (Eitzen and Zinn, 1994).

This chapter uses a **social disorganization theory** for viewing problems associated with infancy. This theory is only one of many social perspectives that could be applied to children in the first years of life. Since infants are dependent on other people and systems for their very survival, a social disorganization framework seems particularly appropriate for analyzing this developmental phase.

The previous chapter stated that social systems are comprised of various social elements, including social roles, groups, organizations, institutions (e.g., the family and the economic structure), communities, and states (Meenaghan and Washington, 1980, pp. 3–5). However, because of social or cultural advancements and changes, some systems change at a slower or faster rate than others. Change results in disequilibrium and social disorganization within the social system and related systems.

An examination of early sociological thought is useful in understanding social disorganization theory. Sociologists August Comte and Herbert Spencer espoused an "organismic" interpretation of society and social structure. They proposed that society and social systems are analogous to biological organisms. Spencer suggests that in both societies and organisms:

1. Growth and development are major themes.
2. Increases in size result in increased differentiation and complexity.
3. Increase in differentiation of structure results in differentiation of function.
4. Parts of the whole are interrelated and interdependent with a change in one part affecting other parts.
5. Each part of the whole is a social unit or organism itself.
6. While the whole can perish the parts of the whole can live. (Turner, 1974, pp. 16–17)

Using what is defined in sociology as a **functionalist perspective**, Spencer and others promote social system equilibrium and stability. Instead of explaining social structures as static, passive, and unchanging, functionalists tend to stress survival of social units and their ability to produce a state of **homeostasis** or balance for the whole and its various parts.

For functionalists, social disorganization, whether due to social change, conflict, or innovation, is often viewed as problematic or pathological, while social order and harmony are perceived as more desirable. For social work practice, this view often requires identifying which system(s) in a social structure is producing social disorganization.

As an example, early social scientists in the United States utilized a social disorganization framework to focus on the processes of industrialization and urbanization and their relationships to social dysfunction in larger cities. Indeed, one could trace the origins of sociology and the profession of social work in the United States to concerns over rapid social change and the emergence of social problems in Boston, New York City, Chicago, Los Angeles, and other large urban centers.

Fundamental to the functionalist perspective is the premise that social structures are organized and maintained by adherence to common ideologies, beliefs, expectations, and rules. This framework creates **social integration** in social units. When social disorganization begins to take place, these binding beliefs and rules are often challenged and may be discarded. According to Julian and Kornblum (1986), social disorganization can result in one of three conditions: normlessness, culture conflict, and breakdown. **Normlessness** refers to a state where rules to guide behavior are not evident. **Culture conflict** involves the presence of contradictory rules with regard to acceptable behavior. **Breakdown** occurs when "obedience to a set of rules results in no reward or in punishment" (Julian and Kornblum, 1986, p. 13).

In summary, a social disorganization theory focuses on the consequences that occur when a "social system, or some part or parts of it, becomes disorganized, with the result that the system operates less effectively" or malfunctions (McKee and Robertson, 1975, p. 14). Underlying most social disorganization is some form of rapid social change that frequently disturbs social norms and expectations and subsequently disrupts the social structure.

DEVELOPMENTAL ISSUES

Developmental literature examining infancy has traditionally focused on physiological and psychological maturation. Havighurst (1952), for example, suggested that walking, taking solid foods, controlling body wastes, learning to relate to others, and the development of simple concepts of physical and social reality are key tasks during the first two years of life.

From a sociological viewpoint, growth, maturation, and well-being during infancy are contingent upon the influence of various social systems. Typically for infants, these systems would include caregivers—such as a parent(s), relatives, day care providers, the family, and health care professionals and providers—social programs, courts, and employers, as well as social institutions providing economic, familial, political, educational, and religious sustenance. Systemic changes or disturbances in one or more of these systems produce multiple effects for individual infants.

While social workers often readily recognize the influence on clients of caregivers, the family, and employers, changes in society as a whole and in social institutions as mentioned above are not as obvious. In the following sections, we examine implications for infants of family, economic, and political institutions.

The Changing Family

We begin our examination of larger social systems by focusing on the American family. Research journals, as well as popular media and political commentators, recently have focused the attention of the nation upon the crises of the American family. While it is important not to blame a single institution for societal decay, the transformation of the family has broad implications for all Americans, especially infants.

Segalman and Himelson suggest:

> The lack of effective family life is one major factor in the creation of a dysfunctional society. This is true in any of the phases of modernization, whether it is in North America, or South America, Africa, Europe, or Asia. Family life appears to be the major element in the creation of what Durkheim called "social solidarity," where people are positively connected to each other. (1994, p. 56)

The family as an institution is not easy to define. Such definitions usually begin with procreation, the regulation of sexual behavior, and the care and socialization of children. The definition and functions of the family are frequently clouded by one's family experiences and cultural values.

For many years, social scientists conceptualized the family in terms of either an extended or nuclear unit. The **extended family** is commonly defined as several generations of relatives living in close physical proximity. Here, aunts, uncles, grandparents, and cousins are active participants in the daily lives of parents and children. Today, this form of family is most often associated with agrarian societies and rural or economically isolated segments in the United States. A distinct advantage of this type of structure involves a familial division of labor for child rearing as well as broader social and material support for infants, children, and parents.

Conversely, the **nuclear family** is a more independent unit consisting of a married couple and their dependent children living away from their relatives. The nuclear family in industrialized societies has greater geographical mobility, which is made possible by advanced transportation. A benefit of the nuclear family includes its smaller size and adaptability to changing conditions. This family configuration is capable of acquiring more resources for its members as a result of its geographical flexibility with increased accessibility to job opportunities. Moreover, in industrialized societies that afford both parents participation in the labor force, there is an immediate need for more formalized day care arrangements for infants and children.

Family patterns of the 1990s, however, have begun to impact our perception of the American family. As single parenting becomes more prevalent and divorce rates approach one out of every two marriages (60 percent of divorcing couples have children), the image of the American family as a stable unit appears mythical. Even with the recent decline of the divorce rate, the institution of the family in America has been radically changed.

While politicians focus on traditional family values, they seem unaware that family structure in America is changing rapidly. With macro awareness, social workers will be active in creating a more comprehensive view of family needs.

Infants in the United States are now born into a high-tech, fast-paced society that lacks a shared definition of family. The term **dual worker families** describes the situation in which both husband and wife are employed. Like single-parent families, dual-worker families face the absence of supports from the workplace and other community resources that could enable spouses to better cope with being both a parent and a worker. And while marriage in the United States is still predicated on the notion of love and commitment, parents often appear to perform more as an economic unit, working together to secure goods in the same physical dwelling, than as two people dedicated to sharing a life together based on mutual aspirations and affection.

Byng-Hall (1995) suggests that emotional attachments lie at the heart of family life. For infants to grow and be nurtured, the family needs to be acting primarily as an emotional unit. A secure family base is provided when a reliable network of attachment relationships are present. Regardless of the composition of the family unit, infants and children require relationships between caregiving adults that are "sufficiently collaborative" to ensure that infants sense care and security in their development (Byng-Hall, 1995, p. 45).

Daka-Mulwanda, Thornburg, Filbert, and Klein (1995) expand the concept of collaborative relationships to include the cooperation and coordination of services for infants and children. Infants and parents can best be served by the integration of federal and state government agencies with community-based services and organizations. This integration can be accomplished through shared philosophies, leadership, funding efforts, and the pooling of resources.

One of child welfare's greatest challenges is to become family centered (Cole, 1995). How can social workers shift from a mentality of rescuing children to a philosophy of strengthening families? **Family preservation services**, a term often used to describe efforts by social service agencies to help keep families intact, has evoked mixed reactions and is sometimes criticized for risking endangerment of the child.

Cole (1995) suggests that early intervention toward producing stability and support for all families promotes their healthy development. Cole (1995, p.167) identifies the goals of family preservation services as:

1. Keeping children and families safe,
2. Improving family functioning to avoid unnecessary placement of children, and
3. Improving the placement process for children, with an emphasis on facilitating reunification of the family.

When the U.S. Congress passed the Family Preservation Act of 1993, a legislative mandate and nearly $1 billion over a five-year period were given to enable states to focus on integrating family support and preservation services. Various states have followed this mandate by beginning Family First initiatives and single-point-of-entry programs. Their objective is to place stability of the family and quality of life for children as top priorities.

One of the more important problems challenging parents of infants in the United States is the need in this industrialized society for a more adequate child care system—in both quality and coverage. The increasing number of single parents and dual-wage-earner families has produced a structural demand for high-quality child care services, yet few industries and businesses provide this for their employees.

While relatives—often grandparents—and day care centers address part of the need for child care, low-income and disadvantaged families often utilize family day care. **Family day care** can be defined as "providers, generally women, who take children into their own homes for a few hours to an entire day. It differs significantly from day care centers in size, personnel, curriculum, physical setting, and atmosphere" (Frankel, 1994, p. 550). Another aspect of family day care even more frequently used is that of in-home child care—babysitters, who are often relatives or neighbors.

The Children's Foundation (1990) has estimated that nearly 5.5 million children in the United States are being served by family day care. While all 50 states have some form of regulation of family day care, there are excellent as well as disastrous examples to be found in public, private, and family day care. Frankel asks several important questions with regard to state licensing, certification, and registration requirements that monitor child care services:

1. Do regulation requirements promote quality family day care?
2. How are regulations enforced?
3. How does family day care come under regulation?
4. Are national standards necessary? (1994, p. 552)

If we are committed to family preservation services, how can child care services be delivered in a manner that strengthens the overall family? Carol Williams, Associate Commissioner of the Children's Bureau, places child care in a primary position in family preservation. "We see child care as a part of a hub, a network in the continuum of services in the community...critical places where families can be linked to other resources" Carroad (1994, p.15). There are continuing concerns, however, that social work services are too brief under most of these programs to rehabilitate a family. Which goal is uppermost—protection of the child or continuation of the family unit? In abusive situations, this question is paramount and requires input from many disciplines.

Based on our brief examination of the American family, several macro system insights for social workers intervening on behalf of infants have emerged. First, there is no generally accepted definition of a family. Second, while the structure of the family in the United States is changing, infants require safe and secure environments to help ensure proper nurture and growth. Finally, family support and preservation services protect and nurture infants. These services impact society both directly and indirectly. "If the family is absent, fragmented, dysfunctional, or powerless, then the socialization of its children will lead to weak, ineffectual, parasitic or antisocial adults" (Segalman and Himelson, 1994, p. 58).

The Changing Economy

Central to all of human experience and present-day society is the principle of work. From the time of simple hunting and gathering to today's industrial age, societies have organized to produce goods and services that provide sustenance, clothing, and shelter to those who participate. Parents provide for their offspring through the structure of work instituted by the social system in which they live. At the same time, socioeconomic inequality is created through the rewards available to workers. The degree to which parents provide for their children is contingent upon earning power in the socioeconomic system, whether it is the result of participation in the labor force or inheritance.

The U.S. work world is typically described in terms of its capitalistic philosophy, high-tech environment, and leadership in the global marketplace. In the midst of a structural transformation "from an industrialized society to an information/ service economy" (Eitzen and Zinn, 1994, p. 431), a highly automated U.S. economy often struggles in its effort to utilize a steady supply of job seekers. The result is **structural**

unemployment, which occurs when there are more people available for work than there are jobs.

The financial circumstances of parents with infants are the major focus of this section. How do general changes in employment opportunities and working conditions in the United States impact young children? Who are the working poor and the poverty stricken? Who feels the brunt of change in America when economic tides shift?

We need to be familiar with some of the language of corporate America in order to set the tone for our inquiry concerning current trends in the U.S. economy. The following tongue-in-cheek phrases and words are from *Fortune* magazine's "Cliched Corporate Conversations from Hell." These sarcastic definitions are directly from The Devil's Dictionary (*Fortune*, 1995, p. 22).

> **Team Player** An employee who substitutes the thinking of the herd for his own good judgment.
>
> **Reengineering** The principal slogan of the Nineties, used to describe any and all corporate strategies.
>
> **Vision** Top management's heroic guess about the future, easily printed on mugs, T-shirts, posters, and calendar cards.
>
> **Paradigm shift** A euphemism companies use when they realize the rest of their industry has expanded into Guangdong while they were investing in Orange County.
>
> **Restructuring** A simple plan instituted from above in which workers are right-sized, downsized, surplused, lateralized, or in the business jargon of days of yore, fired.
>
> **Empowerment** A magic wand management waves to help traumatized survivors of restructuring suddenly feel engaged, self managed, and in control of their futures and their jobs.

Granted, these definitions represent a cynical commentary on the state of thinking in corporate America. Yet, *Fortune*'s glossary of terms suggests that economic life is organized, real, and changing, and includes its own distinct language. Corporate restructuring and downsizing is a trend in American business affecting numerous jobs. And while the moves are not always referred to as paradigm shifts, companies often fail to expand in developing marketplaces or they mistakenly concentrate efforts on saturated markets.

The relationship between employment opportunities for clients with infants and processes such as corporate restructuring, paradigm shifts, and visioning is a concern for all social workers. Changes in the economy affect more than profit taking; they directly impact the lives of people. If parents are unable to find work, experience a decline in wages, or are displaced from the labor force, they will be forced to rely on welfare programs or to seek help elsewhere.

These labor market factors are commonly cited by married women with children as reasons for entering welfare, whereas "widowed, divorced or separated women were more likely to cite family structure changes as reasons for entering welfare" (Leahy, Buss, and Quane, 1995, p. 41). Over 75 percent of the respondents in the study by Leahy and colleagues indicated that their ability to leave welfare was a result of increased earnings or increased earnings of a spouse.

Many studies mistakenly identify divorce as the major cause of women's poverty. These "analyses fail to recognize that it is the visibility of women's unequal access to independent resources, primarily employment income, that divorce reveals" (Pulkingham, 1995, p. 7). Interestingly, U.S. Commerce Department data reveal that while "women in general and white women in particular experienced increasing employment opportunities and rising wages in the 1970's and 1980's...income gains black men experienced in the 1970's declined markedly in the 1980's" (Caputo, 1995, p. 239). Nevertheless, across the board, women continue to earn less than men in jobs and professions.

It is misleading to evaluate or assess the ability of a parent or parents to support an infant child solely on the basis of the number of jobs available at a given time period. Instead, gender and race are salient structural factors when considering employment opportunity and the ability to secure higher paying middle- and upper-class jobs in the American economy. Edin (1991) indicates that the economy strongly affects behavior: When parents, usually women, are pushed to participate in welfare programs, they will engage in whatever actions they deem economically necessary to provide for their children. They may conceal from their welfare worker both outside income and financial assistance from family members or the absent father. Most important, "mothers stayed on welfare because they could not find jobs" (Edin, 1991, p. 462), particularly jobs that would make them independent with more disposable income for their family. Edin's research illustrates that women who rely on public assistance to provide for children are both resilient and resourceful.

While their struggle would appear to be emotionally and psychologically stressful, women receiving public assistance can exhibit considerable growth. Despite economic hardships and being on welfare, an improved self-identity, supportive friends, new experiences, and certain government programs such as Medicaid and rent subsidies contributed to making the women healthier, more productive, and more confident (Nesto, 1994, p. 244).

Readers are cautioned to resist the temptation to view economic opportunities for parents with children in a piecemeal or program-by-program manner over large-scale systemic change. It is often simpler to focus exclusively on specific policies and programs such as child support enforcement (Oellerich, Garfinkel, and Robins, 1991) or parental leave plans that benefit infants than to attack the core of economic oppression.

Goldberg reminds us that "childhood poverty in this country ought to be setting off national alarms" (1995, p. 47). While programs like the Special Supplemental Feeding Program for Women, Infants, and Children (WIC) have been very successful in addressing nutritional needs of low-income pregnant women, infants, and children, "poverty reduction rather than WIC expansion must be our primary goal" (Goldberg, 1995, p. 47). And how that is to be accomplished continues to puzzle administrators of the program. Though WIC is an excellent program, it serves only a small percentage of women and children eligible for services.

To summarize, the family of the 1990s in America lives in a high-technology, service-oriented economy characterized by structural unemployment, a demand for highly skilled jobs, and utilization of part-time workers. Our brief consideration of the economic institution reveals several factors influencing the ability of parents to provide for infants in the United States. Among these are the types of jobs present in the labor force, availability of employment opportunities, corporate restructuring and visioning, global economic interdependence, and the systematic oppression of people based on race and gender.

The Political Process

Do you vote? Can you name the U.S. senators from your state or the congressperson serving your district? Are you familiar with the various state senators and representatives charged with formulating laws in your state? Who are the leaders of your state and local executive branches, your governor, your mayor? Who are the judges that interpret and act upon law in various federal, state, and local jurisdictions?

If you had difficulty in answering these questions, you are probably not alone. Many Americans struggle in their attempt to understand the political system in the United States and to keep abreast of political trends and current legislation. Yet, the political institution of a society performs important functions. Political systems, through the establishment of government, enable societies to establish social control, develop norms and laws, produce economic security, set priorities, provide for the common good, and equip for defense from outside dangers. Moreover, votes on health and entitlement policies and programs benefiting infants and children often are determined by political ideologies and alliances.

In general, **politics** can be defined as "the process that determines which groups of people or individuals exercise power over others" (Tischler, 1990, p. 490). Weber's classic definition of **power** highlights the ability of one person or group to carry out their will over others. The stakes are high when a particular person, group, or party takes political office. Government leaders have power. Sanctioned by their position, which was acquired by election, coup, or appointment, government officials have the ability to make decisions that impact large numbers of people of all ages.

Political debate of the 1990s centers on welfare reform and, in particular, on the overhaul or recasting of Aid to Families with Dependent Children (AFDC). With respect to welfare reform, Meyer states, "American politics is preoccupied with the budgetary deficit, with lowering taxes, with downsizing government, and with other economic priorities...but the government is not a profit-making corporation—it is supposed to provide for the public's well-being. When money is tight, why not cut the programs that serve those who are least able to join in protest?" (1994, p. 229). Women who are single parents, as well as infants and children relying on government programs, are easy political prey when compared to bank officials seeking refuge from faltering savings and loan associations, or corporate heads and stockholders prospering from Pentagon spending. The fact that children do not vote is not lost upon those in elected offices.

Zinsmeister states, "The 1994 electoral revolt against big government was no unconsidered jerk of the knee" (1995, p. 16). Americans perceive big government as one of our country's most critical concerns, presumably even if favoring smaller government means fewer services. The politically conservative argue that the 1994 landslide election of Republicans to the U.S. Congress reflects both a general disdain for government intervention into individuals' lives and a public endorsement of the now famous "Contract with America" aimed at reducing federal government spending and curtailing social programs.

The National Association of Social Workers (NASW), however, gave the "Contract with America" failing marks. NASW President Sheldon Goldstein stated, "The American people are saying that this isn't what they signed up for.... We give the

'Contract' a resounding 'F' for failing to provide for America's children and families" (NASW, 1995, p. 1). The NASW indicates that provisions in the "Contract" would have denied benefits to over 6 million children, reduced food stamps and child care support for working families, and undermined family and medical leave policies as well as child labor laws. Liberals argue that the "Contract" is mean spirited and an attempt to balance the federal budget by reducing benefits to the poor while the wealthy prosper.

Our brief glimpse into the political system in America is intended to raise awareness of the crucial role of governmental leaders. Support for social programs benefiting infants correlates closely with the priorities of individuals, groups, or parties in political power. As political winds shift, government support for young children changes. It is important for social workers to analyze and participate in the political environment in which they practice.

The social worker–client relationship is immersed in politics whenever the executive branch enforces the law, a legislative branch makes laws, or the judicial system interprets them.

CASE EXAMPLE

Mrs. Clara Sherman, a 36-year-old African-American woman, is the newly appointed executive director of the Infants' Milk Fund and Prenatal Clinic (IMFPC) located in a large city in the western United States. Clara received her Master of Social Work degree in 1987 with a concentration in clinical social work. She has worked at the IMFPC for the past six years as a social worker and then as a supervisor of social workers.

While in graduate school, Clara also completed several courses in supervision and administration. Her faculty advisor was aware of research indicating the increasing number of MSW graduates entering supervisory positions (Skidmore, 1990, p. 10), so she recommended these courses in anticipation of Clara's entry into an administrative position in social work.

Since graduation, Clara has continued to develop her knowledge base and skills in administration through graduate course work and specialized workshops.

In her new position at the IMFPC, Clara provides leadership in providing prenatal and pediatric services to high-risk, low-income mothers and infants. Services offered at the IMFPC include immunization, an early detection and screening program, monitoring of growth and development of infants, preventive health care, psychosocial intervention, and both prenatal and pediatric care clinics. In addition, the IMFPC sponsors a newborn outreach program that serves to link the IMFPC, the WIC program, and community pediatric caregivers. The IMFPC is a United Way agency and employs social workers, nurses, pediatricians, medical assistants, and clerical support staff.

As a new director, Clara faces many challenges. Last year, under her direction, the social work staff at the IMFPC (two MSWs and two BSWs) conducted a comprehensive needs assessment for the service area. One goal of the assessment was to identify population groups within the scope of the agency that were not being served or were underserved. Findings indicated that a growing number of women in the community were diagnosed with severe mental illness. Many of the subjects of this study who were mothers of infants needed the services of IMFPC. These women had little knowledge in the areas of feeding, nutrition, developmental milestones, and practical information regarding the care of infants.

The suburban area served by the IMFPC is characterized by both economic and urban decline. The relocation of a major transportation center, the revitalization of the nearby downtown business district, and an increasing crime rate have resulted in suburban flight by longtime residents of the neighborhood. Those remaining have fallen even lower on the poverty scale. In addition, the national trend toward deinstitutionalization of the mentally disabled has made this section of the city a haven for persons with mental illness living alone.

Coincidentally, the IMFPC needs-assessment and a recent community plan assessment completed by the local mental health association produced similar results in describing a profile of women and infants requiring prenatal and pediatric services. A profile of women in need of IMFPC assistance highlighted several characteristics: most were in their early twenties, predominantly white, living in some form of private housing. They had been hospitalized on an average of two times during the past five years and continue to receive psychotropic medication. They were marginally employed, and were involved in a romantic relationship but remained unmarried. A large percentage were participating in case management services provided by the county mental health association.

Clara and the social work staff convinced the board of directors of the IMFPC that this segment of the community is being underserved and will require special programming. While empathetic, the IMFPC board is concerned about federal cutbacks in funding, particularly since over 60 percent of the funding for IMFPC comes from Medicaid and Medicaid Managed Care funding.

TIME TO THINK!

In this case example, Clara Sherman is a social worker executing an administrative role in macro practice. She is exerting organizational leadership by identifying and articulating future directions whereby her agency can address a community need (Brody and Nair, 1995). Clara's client system entails a specific population of women and infants. What macro-level issues are raised here? How should they be prioritized? Does Clara's employment as a social work administrator impose an increased need to assess and utilize macro-level systems? If so, why?

MACRO SYSTEMS AND WOMEN WITH SEVERE MENTAL ILLNESS AND THEIR INFANTS

As previously emphasized, a major focus of this book involves the inclusion of macro systems and issues for assessing problems in social work practice. Our intent is to demonstrate how this emphasis transcends the specific role in which a social worker is employed. In the following sections, consider the organizational, community, societal, and global factors that could act to facilitate or inhibit the creation of special prenatal and pediatric programming for women with severe mental illnesses.

Organizational Level

As the chief administrator at the IMFPC, Clara Sherman is active in planning, coordinating, and evaluating various aspects of organizational life to help her agency define and achieve its goals. Thus, she has a clear vision of the IMFPC's mission and objectives. Clara knows the structure of the IMFPC, where the locus of power lies, the resources available, and how internal processes operate. Clara has thoroughly analyzed the strengths and limitations of her own organization for providing prenatal and pediatric care.

Clara has also benefited from her experience in providing direct service to women and infants at the IMFPC. Over the years, as a case manager and later as a social work administrator, Clara collected information from and nurtured contacts with many important social service organizations. These included the local mental health center, the county mental health association and board, the Association for the Mentally Ill (AMI), children's services, many local health care providers, the county commissioners office, city hall, and various advocacy and crisis centers for women.

Clara firmly believes that successful program development at the IMFPC aimed at providing service for women with severe mental illness will require input and a collaborative effort from many, if not all, of the aforementioned organizations. For Clara and her staff, contacting key individuals and organizing meetings to assess common interests and goals for developing a program of intervention with this population will be essential. Clara is very aware of the financial hardships currently facing social service organizations and is realistic as she considers the ability of funding sources to finance new programs.

In her quest to appraise the willingness of various organizations to pursue prenatal and pediatric services for women with severe mental illness, Clara has also not forgotten the perspective of the consumer and the importance of client input in all phases and aspects of social work practice. Whether it represents individual clients or organized associations of clients, the voice of the consumer in assessing problems and planning interventions is imperative. Clients with severe mental illness are strongly empowered when they take actions that improve their own life situations.

By regular study of the most recent research, Clara is aware that gender differences exist when assessing viable social networks for persons with severe mental illness. Walsh (1994) suggests that men with severe mental illness are more likely to participate in task-oriented and recreational organizations like the YMCA, the community center, and clubs, whereas women with severe mental illness are more likely to remain with relatives and non-task-oriented friends in neighborhoods and social groups. These findings are particularly important in shaping the form and structure of any prenatal or pediatric program designed for women with severe mental illness.

Community Level

The IMFPC is located in a community experiencing rapid social change. Once a thriving suburb, the area is now characterized by low-income housing, high unemployment, and high crime. Many of these changes can be attributed to an economic downturn in this part of the city. Last year a major airport serving the western half of the United States was closed and relocated to another section of town. Meanwhile, city officials have spent millions of dollars to modernize the adjacent downtown business district, climaxed by the opening of a new major league baseball stadium, with little attention directed toward the community served by the IMFPC.

For businesses that have remained in the community, vandalism, theft, and other forms of crime have become the norm. As an example, local pizza franchises no longer deliver, and after dark often require customers to pick up pizza orders via drive-through windows. This is intended to protect employees and customers from theft and physical harm.

Because rent is cheap, single parents as well as other people struggling financially have become residents in the community. Indeed, the IMFPC and other social service agencies have seen their client rolls and waiting lists climb as the community has become increasingly impoverished.

Fortunately, a stalwart faction in the community has been an ecumenical coalition of local congregations. Consistent with Harris's findings (1995), this religious coalition, along with many individual congregations, has quietly worked on various human welfare projects in the community including the refurbishing of houses, fund-raising activities, informal care that links individuals for social support and accomplishment of simple tasks, and the promotion of support groups, including a group for parents with infants. Religious congregations have served an important function in the community by providing stability and an increased sense of security.

Gainful employment for her clients is one of Clara's greatest concerns. Clients repeatedly express their desire to work. However, with the recent relocation of the airport, jobs are very difficult to find. Fulfilling work aspirations for women with severe mental challenges who are attempting to nurture infant children is particularly demanding. Successful job placement is a time-consuming endeavor requiring a careful assessment of the strengths of each client and realistic employment opportunities for the severely mentally disabled in the community (Tice, 1994).

Societal Level

How do people in the United States view women who seek economic assistance for their infant children? Meyer describes the current political assault on women on welfare (AFDC) as a "paradigm for the oppression of women—1994 style" (1994, p. 231). For many social workers, the mid-1990s appear to be a dark time in U.S. history as politicians and legislative representatives, in the goal of reestablishing their definition of traditional family values, seek to overemphasize individual responsibility in social policy.

Yet many Americans fully concur with a popular outlook that views women with infants on welfare as societal parasites. Several years ago, House Speaker Newt Gingrich advocated for the return of orphanages for needy children as well as a severing of parental rights if parents were unable to nurture and provide for their children.

For people with mental illness, myths and stereotypes continue to abound in the United States. These persons are often viewed as dangerous and a threat to society (Davis, 1991). Such images further discrimination, often serving to inhibit both housing and employment initiatives for the mentally ill.

When considering establishing a prenatal and pediatric program serving economically deprived women with mental illness, Clara joins forces with other professionals in contemplating how to best educate society to the plight of both the mentally ill and women with dependent children. While some people in our society will be empathetic toward helping small children, they may still regard the mothers of those children with suspicion and anger. Many have come to believe that mental illness is either a fabrication or a disease requiring hospitalization.

On a positive note, Orlin states "During the past 20 years the United States has experienced a public policy revolution affecting people with disabilities" (1995, p. 223). The passage of the Americans with Disabilities Act of 1990 (ADA) signaled monumental federal legislation mandating action to eliminate discrimination against individuals with disabilities. Clara will assess the implications of the ADA for her agency and determine if any ADA service mandates apply to mothers and infants being served at the IMFPC. These mandates are particularly salient with respect to any future programs for clients diagnosed as severely mentally ill.

Clara's involvement with PACE, the NASW's political action committee, allows her to be informed of new legislation relevant to mentally ill women with young children. She then can be proactive in sharing her concerns with legislators and in advocating for her agency's clientele. Clara also meets monthly with her local representative from the state legislature to share insights that will advance employment opportunities for mothers experiencing mental illness.

International Level

The American welfare state is approaching a crisis as a result of current trends in the global economy (Karger, 1991). Corporations, forced to vie for profits in a highly competitive world marketplace, implement policies emphasizing efficiency. These policies spur plant shutdowns, industrial reorganization, and the implementation of advanced technology.

Additionally, to assist corporations to become more profitable, the government often curtails taxes and creates economic incentives to make capital available to corporations for investment. These forms of government support of business and industry may be defined as **corporate welfare**. The net economic outgrowth of this subsidy is increased government debt and a reduction in welfare spending.

People seeking employment in this environment see long-term employees being replaced by part-time, temporary, and lower-paid workers. Even as a member of a professional, managerial, or technical group, an unemployed person may become a participant in a "floating population" of workers moving from job to job in pursuit of better salary and benefits, with little personal attachment or stake in her or his current employment.

For Clara, these employment practices are very familiar. In working with low-income mothers with infants, Clara sees a national trend toward reducing welfare services and benefits. Not only are the available jobs low paying and temporary, but

Clara's clients compete with high school and college students for these positions. Ironically, few seem to be offended by the fact of competition for funds between government support of business and industry and the services providing the assistance to which they might be entitled.

Conversely, others take a far less grim approach in analyzing global trends in relationship to the economy and welfare in the United States. "Despite our current economic problems, our share of the world economy has remained nearly constant for the past quarter of a century...poverty in America is viewed as comfortable living in 90 percent of the world" (Kando, 1992, pp. 32–33).

Kando (1992) encourages Americans to be optimistic about global trends. When analyzing the world economy and international issues, liberals often take a doomsday approach, seeing only decline and negativity while failing to recognize the many positive conditions in America.

Clara, as director of the IMFPC, realizes that many infants in other parts of the world do not receive nutrition, medical care, and various forms of support of the quality provided in the United States. Yet, means of survival and standards of living are relative concepts. Clara's quest is to determine how to provide the best prenatal and pediatric care possible for expectant mothers and infants, using American standards.

APPLYING A SOCIAL WORK FRAMEWORK: SOCIAL DISORGANIZATION THEORY

At the beginning of this chapter a social disorganization perspective was introduced. Fundamental to an understanding of social disorganization theory is the premise that a social structure is comprised of various systems that are interrelated and interdependent. When change occurs in one system, changes take place in other parts of the whole. From this orientation, social structures, much like human organisms, strive to survive and establish a sense of balance or homeostasis.

In our case example, Clara Sherman stays abreast of modifications in other systems that could impact her agency. Over the years, it has become increasingly apparent to Clara that changes occurring at all social levels have affected life at the IMFPC. Several of the more significant societal revolutions include a high divorce rate and the rapid growth of the single-parent family in the United States, a restructuring of corporate America and the American workforce, and the recent political turn toward less government with greater emphasis on individual responsibility. Within the neighborhood served by the IMFPC, a high rate of unemployment and underemployment has resulted in increased poverty and a rise in demand for social services.

Using a social disorganization perspective, Figueira-McDonough concludes that when communities experience high rates of poverty they "will have high levels of social disorganization in the domains of work, family, and community detachment" (1995, p. 63). Changes in the economy, family structure, politics, education, and religion impact the IMFPC program. What meaning will these changes have upon the agency's efforts to service mentally ill mothers? While Clara is uncertain as to which of them functions as the motor propelling social disorganization, she strives to understand the significance of these changing institutions.

When assessing organizational life from a social disorganization perspective, Clara has learned that the IMFPC does not operate in a vacuum. A swing of the political pendulum, a turn in the economy, or a twist in family structures will influence the functioning of Clara's agency and the lives of her clients. At times Clara's job seems overwhelming as she tries to keep up to date and knowledgeable about a dynamic and changing social environment.

SUGGESTED ACTIVITIES
---

1. Using a discussion group format, examine issues related to day care for infants in America. What five factors would influence your decision regarding day care? How many day care facilities are available within a three-mile radius of your home?

2. Contact the officer of a local labor union to observe a meeting, rally, or gathering. Are unemployment, restructuring of the labor force, or corporate welfare referred to directly or obliquely? What union programs are family-friendly and responsive to the health and welfare of young children?

3. Observe a city council meeting in your hometown or legislative assembly session. If this is impractical, you may choose to watch a congressional session on C-Span via cable television. Analyze the political rhetoric and identify the group of people or constituency each member appeals to or represents. Would you consider the speaker to be in support of social policies and programs for families and children? Why or why not?

——————— REFERENCES ———————

Andrejevic, M. (1995). Michigan Babies Get Healthier. *Lansing State Journal*, June 24, 1-2.

Brody, R., & Nair, M. (1995). *Macro Practice: A Generalist Approach.* Wheaton, IL: Gregory Publishing Company.

Byng-Hall, J. (1995). Creating a Secure Family Base: Some Implications of Attachment Theory for Family Therapy. *Family Process*, 34(1), 45-58.

Caputo, D. (1995). Gender and Race: Employment Opportunity and the American Economy, 1969-1991. *Families in Society: The Journal of Contemporary Human Services*, 76(4), 239-247.

Carroad, D. (1994). Key Child Care and Other Federal Programs for Infants and Toddlers. *Children Today*, 23(2), 14-36.

Children's Foundation (1990). *The Children's Foundation: Providing Practical Answers to Tough Questions Since 1969.* Washington, DC.

Cole, E. (1995). Becoming Family Centered: Child Welfare's Challenge. *Families in Society: The Journal of Contemporary Human Services*, 76(3), 163-172.

Combs-Orme, T., Risley-Curtiss, C., & Taylor, R. (1993) Predicting Birth Weight: Relative Importance of Sociodemographic, Medical, and Prenatal Care Variables. *Social Service Review*, 67(4), 617-630.

Daka-Mulwanda, V., Thornburg, K., Filbert, L., & Klein, T. (1995). Collaboration of Services for Children and Families. *Family Relations*, 44(2), 219-223.

Davis, S. (1991). An Overview: Are Mentally Ill People Really More Dangerous? *Social Work*, 36(2), 174-180.

Edin, K. (1991). Surviving the Welfare System: How AFDC Recipients Make Ends Meet in Chicago. *Social Problems*, 38(4), 462-474.

Eitzen, D., & Zinn, M. (1994). *Social Problems.* Boston: Allyn and Bacon.

Figueira-McDonough, J. (1995). Community Organization and the Underclass: Exploring New Practice Directions. *Social Service Review*, 69(1), 57-85.

Fortune (1995). Cliched Corporate Conversations from Hell. 131(3), 22.

Frankel, A. (1994). Family Day Care in the United States. *Families in Society: The Journal of Contemporary Human Services*, 75(9), 550-560.

Goldberg, P. (1995). Poverty and Nutrition: If Steinbeck Were Alive Today. *Families in Society: The Journal of Contemporary Human Services*, 76(1), 46-49.

Harris, M. (1995). Quiet Care: Welfare Work and Religious Congregations. *Journal of Social Policy*, 24(1), 53-71.

Havighurst, R. (1952). *Developmental Tasks and Children*. New York: D. McKay Co.

Julian, J., & Kornblum, Q. (1986). *Social Problems*. Englewood Cliffs, NJ: Prentice-Hall.

Kando, T. (1992). Is Anything Right About America? *International Journal on World Peace*, 9(1), 31-36.

Karger, H. (1991). The Global Economy and the American Welfare State. *Journal of Sociology and Social Welfare*, 18(1), 3-20.

Leahy, P., Buss, T., & Quane, J. (1995). Time on Welfare: Why Do People Enter and Leave the System? *American Journal of Economics and Sociology*, 54(1), 33-46.

McKee, M., & Robertson, I. (1975). *Social Problems*. New York: Random House.

Meenaghan, T., & Washington, R. (1980). *Social Policy and Social Welfare: Structure and Applications*. New York: The Free Press.

Meyer, C. (1994). The Latent Issues of Welfare Reform. *Affilia*, 9(3), 229-231.

National Association of Social Workers (1995). Report Card Gives Contract Failing Grades. *Ohio Chapter Newsletter*, 19(10), 1.

National Center for Health Statistics (1993). *Health, United States, 1992*. Hyattsville, MD: Public Health Service.

Nesto, B. (1994). Low-Income Single Mothers: Myths and Realities. *Affilia*, 9(3), 232-246.

Newsweek (1992). His Saddest Song, March 23, 52-53.

Oellerich, D., Garfinkel, I., & Robins, P. (1991). Private Child Support: Current and Potential Impacts. *Journal of Sociology and Social Welfare*, 18(3), 3-20.

Orlin, M. (1995). The Americans with Disabilities Act: Implications for Social Services. *Social Work*, 40(2), 233-239.

Pulkingham, J. (1995). Investigating the Financial Circumstances of Separated and Divorced Parents: Implications for Family Law Reform. *Canadian Public Policy*, 21(1), 1-19.

Segalman, R., & Himelson, A. (1994). The Family: Past, Present, and Future. *International Journal of World Peace*, 11(1), 51-64.

Skidmore, R. (1990). *Social Work Administration: Dynamic Management and Human Relationships*. Englewood Cliffs, NJ: Prentice-Hall.

Tice, C. (1994). A Community's Response to Supported Employment: Implications for Social Work Practice. *Social Work*, 39(6), 728-735.

Tischler, H. (1990). *Introduction to Sociology*. New York: Holt, Rinehart and Winston, Inc.

Turner, J. (1974). *The Structure of Sociological Theory*. Homewood, IL: The Dorsey Press.

Walsh, J. (1994). Gender Differences in the Social Networks of Persons with Severe Mental Illness. *Affilia*, 9(3), 247-268.

Weber, M. (1958). Class, Status, and Party. In H. Gerth & C. Mills (Eds.), *Max Weber: Essays in Sociology*. New York: Oxford University Press.

Zinsmeister, K. (1995). Indicators. *The American Enterprise*, 6(2), 16-19.

Zopf, P. (1992). *Mortality Patterns and Trends in the United States*. Westport, CT: Greenwood Press.

3

Preschool Children

A mischievous-looking boy with tousled blonde hair pulls his wagon down the sidewalk. He is wearing bib overalls, tennis shoes, and a striped shirt. He greets his next-door neighbor with a cheerful "Good morning, Mr. Wilson." Mr. Wilson cautiously replies and hides behind his newspaper. In the background Mrs. Mitchell, searching for her son, calls, "Dennis! Dennis!"

Here is the profile of a familiar preschooler—"Dennis the Menace" of television, cartoon, and movie fame. Dennis Mitchell is a lovable and curious preschooler with a penchant for getting into trouble. Though without malice, Dennis has a propensity for making mischief at the most inopportune time. Mr. Wilson, the temperamental next-door neighbor, is often the recipient of Dennis's misbehaviors.

From a developmental perspective, Dennis is experiencing a new and trying period. Now mobile and less confined to his home, Dennis has begun to display a sense of **self**, that is, how he views himself in relationship to other people. Dennis has begun the process of developing his own attitudes, beliefs, and behaviors, and he tests them in various places, especially with Mr. and Mrs. Wilson.

DENNIS the MENACE

" MAYBE I'LL **NEVER** GO TO SCHOOL ... MY FOLKS KEEP TELLIN' ME NOT TO BE SO SMART. "

DENNIS THE MENACE® used by permission of Hank Ketcham and © by North America Syndicate

The image Dennis presents is that of an energetic, playful, and active little boy. His parents are portrayed as reserved, conservative, and faithful to work, family, and home. Given these descriptions, one is left to wonder at the origin of Dennis's troublemaking demeanor. Is this child's behavior typical of most preschoolers? Does Dennis have a personality flaw or conduct disorder? Can his disposition be attributed to his exposure to others in particular social settings? Are we seeing a combination of psychological, behavioral, and social factors? In examining self-image, two considerations are noteworthy. First, what is the role of **inborn directedness** (biological and genetic predispositions and determinants) in the development of self? Second, how important is social interaction for the development of self? **Acquisition after birth** is a term that encompasses all social and environmental factors influencing one's self-concept. From a macro-system perspective, our primary interest concerns the influence of various social systems on the emergence of a child's self-concept.

How do we conceptualize the full meaning of "acquisition after birth" in relationship to the development of self? When considering the complexity of human growth and development, we look for the locus of control. When exposed to different ideas and behaviors, are children able to use intelligence and moral insight to choose between right and wrong or appropriate versus inappropriate behavior? An **internal locus of control** implies that humans are active, assertive beings in the socialization process and are in command of their own actions. Conversely, when children are viewed as passive creatures who are highly vulnerable to the influence of others, an **external locus of control** is evident.

Preschool children are engaged in the process of developing internal mechanisms of control. "Internal expectancies are probably based on a history of learning experiences where variations in one's behavior were followed by predictable variations in reinforcement consequences" (Feld and Radin, 1982, p. 267). Feld and Radin suggest that children who are consistently rewarded for compliant behavior by parents and/or significant others develop internal expectancies defining such behavior as desirable. Conversely, when children receive responses to behaviors that are inconsistent or unpredictable, the locus of control becomes more external as behavior of the child becomes more directly linked to immediate consequences.

Since Dennis the Menace is a fictional character, his self-concept is clearly the result of the writer's pen. In real life, however, how a child views herself or himself is a combination of both inborn directedness and the acquisition of many factors after birth. But when considering where control lies, it is apparent that children are especially vulnerable to information and influence exerted by parents and significant others, as well as television, movies, music, video games, and other technical media.

To compound matters, children are exposed to conflicting messages. Some grow up under joint custody agreements and may find themselves spending extended periods of time in more than one household. Preschool children have little to say in choosing their parents, siblings, playmates, day care arrangements, or neighborhood. Even though parents are conscientious and assertive in influencing their children's socialization, court orders, employment, and other socioeconomic factors limit choices and restrict parental options for child rearing.

From cartoons, television, and movies, Dennis may confirm the impression that some children are born with a predisposition for oppositional, defiant, and troublesome behavior, while other children are inherently obedient and sensitive to the wishes of others. When Mr. Wilson says "That Dennis!" is he condemning Dennis's actions or expressing discouragement with this youngster's personality and lack of internal control?

As social workers, we are challenged to reframe our view of the development of preschoolers using a macro-level approach. Homans (1950), in his classic *The Human Group*, studied factory life and street-gang influence, as well as an entire New England community, to see individuals in relationship to the ongoing processes of social systems. In assessing the actions of preschoolers, individually or as a group, one gains insight by studying the influence of neighborhood, groups, preschools, television, and other related macro-level social systems. Measuring the effect of social forces on a child's self-concept and behavior is a complex process. The understanding of social determinants, as well as psychological and genetic factors, in explaining human behavior is a major challenge in social work practice.

THEORY: SYMBOLIC INTERACTIONISM

Symbolic interactionism is a helpful orientation in examining preschool children. This theory is particularly useful in understanding the world of preschoolers. Because preschoolers are immersed in the development of self, symbolic interaction provides valuable constructs for analyzing this dynamic human process.

Many social work students will characterize symbolic interaction by the familiar adage: I am not who I think I am, and I am not who you think I am, but I am who I think you think I am. This concise, enigmatic sentence captures the essence of Cooley's (1909) **looking-glass self**, a perspective that describes how individuals derive a sense of self through interaction with other people.

As interpreted by Cooley, the self is a social product developed through social interaction. The looking-glass self begins early and continues to be an important determinant, not only during childhood but throughout life. Key elements in the looking-glass self include social interaction, social comparison, reflective appraisals, and self-judgment. When assessing the self definition of a particular child or adult, sources and forms of social interaction and social comparison (e.g., the use of symbols, gestures, and language) are important considerations.

Each of us develops a sense of self based on presumed judgments of significant others (Cooley, 1909). First, through **social comparison** human beings attempt to cognitively understand how their actions appear to others. Next, they receive feedback as to how others have judged or evaluated their behaviors, often referred to as **reflective appraisals**. Finally, individuals make an analysis and judgment of their own behavior based on their perceptions of the feedback provided by others.

George Herbert Mead, a student of Cooley and often credited as the originator of symbolic interactionism, built upon his mentor's work. Mead (1934) gave special attention to specifying a definition of the self and analyzing the origin of the self in childhood. Mead conceptualized self in terms of two distinct parts, the "I" and the "me." Similar to inborn directedness, the **"I"** refers to the spontaneous, biological part of the self that is free from control of others. The "I" is the unique and distinctive side of the self. Conversely, the **"me"** is the social part of self, obtained through socialization with individuals, family, friends, school, and other social entities.

With regard to the development of self, Mead, this pioneer in the study of human development, identified three stages. First, children imitate the behavior of other people, a preparatory stage. Second, children develop the ability to play specific social roles whereby they are able not only to imitate behavior but also to fulfill role expectations, using appropriate language and action. Finally, through games children learn rules that teach appropriate versus inappropriate behavior among various players.

Through participation in games children demonstrate the ability to **take the role of the other**, to envision the expectations of each role in a social system as well as general rules for behaving. As an example, a preschooler playing "Simon Says" learns that there are different expectations for each position (leader and follower), along with a general set of rules for playing the game. Mead extended this logic, asserting that through social comparison children learn broader definitions concerning societal positions, rules, and expectations.

Using symbolic interactionism, people can be compared to players in a game. They "interact in ways that, depending on the course of the interaction, create, maintain, and change the rules of the game" (Turner, 1974, p. 178). From this perspective, human beings are viewed at a more interpersonal level as active participants in both interpreting and changing the social world. While other sociological theories propose that social systems have an existence separate from participants, "interactionists remind us that the educational system, the family, the political system and indeed all of society's institutions are ultimately created, maintained, and changed by people interacting with one another" (Tischler, 1990, p. 25).

DEVELOPMENTAL ISSUES

The preschool period extends from three to six years of age. Topics typically explored in life-span development literature examining preschool children include personality development, gender-role acquisition, play, peer groups, differential socialization of girls and boys, parent-child relationships, preschool facilities, and child care. The focal point of research in the preschool age group has been the relationship between the child and the primary caretaker, traditionally the mother.

The interactionist tenet states that preschool children establish a sense of self and learn appropriate ways of acting in a social system through social interaction. It allows us to identify and examine important macro-level factors with regard to the socialization of preschoolers. In this chapter we will consider the development of preschoolers as related to the detachment of fathers, parental coalitions, children parenting children, day care centers, television, and racism. Each topic is framed in macro-level terms, as a societal trend or a function of the changing American family.

Detached Fatherhood

In 1994 over 12 million children in the United States lived in female-headed households (U.S. Department of Commerce, 1995). This figure raises important questions concerning the relevance of fatherhood. Many agree that "children have the most to gain when living in close association with two parents who are actively involved with the child's development, education, and overall well-being" (Slayton, 1993, p. 24).

When fathers do not assume responsibility for supporting their children financially, psychologically, or socially children are penalized. If a father is absent or disengaged, both the child's emotional development and financial security are jeopardized.

The issue of fatherhood goes beyond providing basic economic and emotional security required for child growth and development. While establishing paternity—as well as the child's rights and entitlements—is an important first step, children require more from parents than the meeting of basic human needs. Prolonged thoughtful and consistent input from parental figures promotes a clearer understanding of age-appropriate behaviors. The child also begins to comprehend that there are societal regulations that govern our actions. Every child benefits from contact with a legally and morally responsible father.

Life without a father is a "leading cause of the decline in the well-being of children...the engine driving our most urgent social problems, from crime to adolescent pregnancy to domestic violence" (Blankenhorn, 1995, p. 6). Blankenhorn further suggests that children in today's society are confused as to what it means to be a man and a father. "Men are increasingly viewed as superfluous to family life: either expendable or part of the problem. Masculinity itself often is treated with suspicion, and even hostility, in our cultural discourse" (Blankenhorn, 1995, p. 6).

Preschool children look to mothers and fathers, as well as significant others, for feedback regarding the appropriateness of their actions. These individuals become **agents for socialization** imparting to children various values and ideals defining a sense of right and wrong for a particular social structure. In this sense, what is normal for a child is dictated by the reactions and feedback from those people interacting closely with the child. Family members and significant others serve to link macro-level community and societal expectations with a child's notion of normality. For example, a child reared in a family where drug culture is the norm will assume that those activities are correct and expected behaviors.

The United States is a society of many cultures. When a child's mother or father are not married or live separate lives, the child may be exposed to very different **cultural values**— prescribed ways of behaving manifested in language, thinking, and expression. Lum (1995) reminds us that "To identify a unique set of values for all ethnic minorities or to claim that all cultures have common values misidentifies the multidimensional levels of culture." It becomes necessary to "strive to differentiate the particular cultural context when addressing the broad theme of cultural values" in early childhood socialization (Lum, 1995, p. 63).

Parental Coalition

Parental coalition occurs when parents successfully form a bond or union for collaboration and coordination about decisions affecting their children. A strong coalition provides uniform rather than mixed messages for children. Recent research suggests that children benefit most when "parents share the same ideas about a child's need for control and guidance." To accomplish this unified approach requires a conscious effort, clear communication, and intentional compromise (Mc Hale, Crouter, Mc Guire, and Updegraff, 1995, p. 126).

Parental coalitions can be established in a variety of family contexts, including divorced, blended, and poverty-stricken families. Those coalitions may be facilitated by public and private programs. Hashima and Amato (1994) suggest the provision of child care from outside the family as a viable societal consideration for reducing problematic behaviors between parents. When parents in poverty have assistance in caring for their children, they are less stressed and more amicable, yielding a more supportive and affectionate family environment.

Increases in single parenthood—most often women raising children alone—custodial grandparents serving as parents, teen parenthood, and gay/lesbian families demand the coordination of all adults performing parental duties. Friends, grandparents, and companions must provide a united front or be the source of conflicting messages and expectations for children in their care. For the children's welfare, steady, positive reinforcement, defining acceptable behavior over unacceptable behavior, creates structure and consistency in life.

In the case of the single parent, demands placed on the preschooler must be steady, dependable, and understandable. Because a preschool child interacts predominantly with one adult is no assurance of consistency or clarity in the presentation of social expectations and norms to the child.

As an example, a single parent, weary and overwhelmed from a full day of work, may retreat from establishing boundaries for her or his child. At times it may seem easier for an exhausted parent to allow the preschooler to disobey a rule or throw a temper tantrum than to generate the energy to intervene.

To assist parents, many communities offer supportive services. Presented under different auspices, these programs provide parents with a forum for expressing mutual support and exchange of ideas. Typically, meetings are held at night with care provided for children.

When Children Parent

Unfortunately, many times children assume the role of parent in caring for younger siblings. Parenting by children often occurs out of necessity and/or default. The result is psychological and physical stress for the children involved.

Children rearing children contributes to difficulties in "forging a workable and coherent identity" as well as perils and "costs of slipping, of saying or doing the wrong thing, or making the wrong choice" (Halpern, 1995, p. 131). Basically, children who assume responsibilities in rearing siblings take on a role they are not intellectually or emotionally prepared to handle. It is neither reasonable nor prudent to expect children to shoulder the duties associated with nurturing and socializing younger sisters or brothers to the expectations and rules associated with family life and society at large.

Day Care Options

Whereas in the second chapter we examined in-home day care options, here we explore the use of day care centers for preschoolers. Most children in day care centers are three or four years old. Teachers in day care centers are predominantly white, under 40 years of age, and have attended college (Whitebook, Howes, and Phillips, 1990).

Advantages of day care centers are their stability and public accountability. Approximately half of the day care centers in the United States operate for profit. The majority are small, single-center enterprises. Compared to other child care arrangements, day care centers usually have staff with child development training, introduce educational materials, offer full day care, and provide structured play time with peers (Clarke-Stewart, Gruber, and Fitzgerald, 1994).

Not surprisingly, the performance of children in day care can be linked directly to the behavior of caregivers (Clarke-Stewart, Gruber, and Fitzgerald, 1994, p. 12). Children tend to imitate actions of teachers, and they quickly learn to incorporate into their repertoire the language, habits, and mannerisms of day care staff members.

When educational programs exist in day care, children tend to spend more time engaged in complex and constructive play. Conversely, when children are left with unstructured playtime with other children and the ratio of adults to children is low, the classroom climate is likely to be less cooperative and more negative. Thus, the key to obtaining high-quality care appears to be "the teacher's degree of attention to, interest, and engagement in the activity of the child" (Thyssen, 1995, p. 91).

Day care centers also have their deficits. They can be noisy, bustling places that overlook the individual needs of the child (Zigler and Lang, 1991). Day care centers can also be expensive, with those families most in need of child care being least able to afford their services (Edelman, 1989).

Child care providers and day care centers are pivotal players in a child's world. A caregiver's activities are not one-dimensional; they include attending to the physical needs of the child as well as creating a rich environment for learning and development (Phillips and Whitebook, 1990, p. 132). The care of younger children and children with special needs requires an even greater output of energy. Unfortunately, as more women have joined the workforce and as single parenthood has produced an unprecedented need, the public sponsorship of day care programs has been grossly inadequate.

"Deciding who is responsible for child care is not like deciding to buy a pair of shoes on some Saturday in November. The decision requires far more than a mere statement of preference, because many complex influences affect the issue" (Deutsch, 1983, p. 10). Selecting an appropriate day care center or child care provider reflects a choice and an assertion concerning personal behavior, family practices, religious views, and individual attitudes. The discreet day care shopper will ask: Are these the kind of people I want to instruct my child? Will the teachers and children at this day care center be a positive influence on my child? Will the day care staff communicate openly with me concerning my child's developmental needs in order to provide a coordinated team effort in socialization? Or, will my child return home with language, ideas, and values I find to be unacceptable?

Social workers are often called upon to assist parents in locating appropriate child care facilities. Various centers are maintained by state and local departments of welfare in low-income areas. Family agencies are frequently resources for referrals to centers and individuals providing quality care. Among those standards set by care centers should be close professional contact with children and parents, adherence to public health standards, low teacher-student ratios, and an open-door visitation policy. Parents should be able to see a mission statement or have articulated to them a philosophy that guides day care activities. A positive image in the community and recommendations by those families who have used the child care program are reliable yardsticks. Community leaders and helping professionals can also be valuable in assisting parents in choosing high-quality day care providers.

Preschoolers and Television

Parents will often reveal that their most restful time is when their preschooler is watching television. The average preschooler watches approximately 28 hours of television per week (Nielsen Media Research, 1990). Over 95 percent of all households have television (Palmer, 1988, p. 4), with commercial and public broadcasting systems providing most programming. Meanwhile, the relatively recent availability of cable and satellite access allows many households to obtain programs originating from countries around the world.

Concerning public broadcasting, Palmer (1988) notes that preschool programs like *Sesame Street* and *Mister Rogers' Neighborhood* have been traditionally well received by children, parents, and sponsors (foundations, corporations, and public television organizations). Yet, public television has been so underfunded that repeat programming has become the norm, with a year-round average of less than ten minutes of new programming each weekday (Palmer, 1988, p. 6). In public broadcasting, due in great part to limited resources, a well-conceived and organized children's program schedule is lacking. The highly publicized 1995 attack on federal subsidies for public broadcasting also served to reduce governmental support for public television in America.

With regard to commercial television programming, children are viewed by television executives as active economic consumers. Most parents are familiar with the cry "Go, go Power Rangers" and the pressure to buy theme clothes and toys. Kline states:

> Programmes such as *He-Man* and *Care Bears* are not scripted as moral parables or even innocent amusements. Character fiction must serve the marketing functions of introducing a new range of personalities into children's

culture, orientating children to this product line, creating a sense of excitement about these characters, and ultimately leading children to want to use those characters in play. Most of the new children's television animations have been created explicitly for selling a new line of licensed goods. It is simply not sufficient for a program to be popular with kids. (1993, p. 280)

Preschoolers and younger children of school age watching television represent not only exploitable but formative minds. One of the dangers is "the child's lack of ability to relate actions, motives and consequences...they may simply imitate the action that they see" on television (Van Evra, 1990, p. 82). An even greater concern arises when children view programs intended for an adult audience. If parents do not assume an active role in selecting, monitoring, and discussing programs, children may be left to bear the full brunt of commercial television's advertising, influence, and control.

Social workers are advised to make "a careful examination of television and its effects," particularly in relation to child welfare and government regulation of television (Lazar, 1994, p. 72). Social workers should be advocates for television without exploitation, joining with other professional associations and consumer action groups. An example of such an opportunity involves legislation mandating a "V-chip" for blocking television shows. The V-chip allows parents to determine the appropriateness of each program for their children and to eliminate the viewing of programs that show excessive violence or sex.

Parents quickly learn the persuasiveness of television commercials upon their children when a simple exchange is made of a generic brand for a highly advertised cereal in its well-known box. Children frequently ask parents to buy breakfast cereals based on television hype, the prizes inside the box, and/or the nature of the box itself. The reader may remember a long-eared rabbit's famous proclamation "Trix are for kids!" or may be familiar with specific brand names of cereals like Fruity Pebbles and Coco Pebbles, taken from popular cartoon characters. Other companies create likable fictional characters such as Captain Crunch to encourage children to request their product.

In terms of television programming for children, "Socially, the problem seems to be that we once saw a special vision of human possibility in television and now that vision appears to have been pushed aside for the sake of business" (Schneider, 1987, p. 4). Schneider further suggests that children should not view television in isolation. Instead, if families watch television programming and commercials together, children can be encouraged by parents to comment about what is seen. Children are influenced by what mom and dad think and say about the shows and products viewed on television.

Consider the potential effects of television with regard to gender stereotyping, particularly for girls. Preschool girls are often portrayed in passive, submissive roles. Girls are presented as clever and pretty, but dependent, while boys are viewed as energetic, strong, and decisive. Parents serve an important function in debunking these media characterizations and role limitations.

While a considerable amount of research has been conducted on the ill effects of television commercials on children, TV advertising "has certain benefits for the child and family" (Schneider, 1987, p. 73). Advertising can prompt children to enter into conversations with adults concerning consumerism and the value and nature of various products. Children can be guided to develop and articulate judgment about television and advertised products, so that they eventually learn to take responsibility for their viewing decisions and buying habits. Ultimately, television can be a positive influence in the emergence of the child's self if parents assist their child in recognizing a diversity of choice and in acquiring the ability to reject or accept programming and products based on their individuality and interests.

Finally, television can be a powerful ally in promoting the welfare of children and in raising awareness of children's rights. As an example, Oprah Winfrey's documentary *Scared Silent: Exposing and Ending Child Abuse* was aired simultaneously on the CBS and NBC television networks, as well as on the Public

Broadcasting Service, with ABC providing a rebroadcast. The National Child Abuse Hotline received over 112,000 calls in the five days following the airing of this documentary (Rowe, 1992). Many of the phone calls were from young children. Oprah's informative presentation demonstrates the power of television to reach out to children in need and to influence their view of the appropriateness of behaviors of other people.

Racism and Child Development

How children interact with persons of different races and creeds is influenced by many factors including family, friends, caretakers, religious instruction, and television.

> The parents are the first members of the larger society in the life of the child. They are members of a social network that may or may not be a part of the social mainstream. They bring their particular skills and the social network attitudes, values, and ways to the task of child care and rearing. Because of the extreme dependency of the child and the important role of the caretaker, the attitudes, values, and ways of the caretaker greatly influence those of the young child. This allows the caretaker to mediate the child's experiences—to give them meaning and to establish their relative importance. (Comer, 1989, pp. 17-18)

While much has been written about gender identification during the preschool years, psychological development of children around the age of three also permits children to begin to differentiate among races and to experience the effects of racism. In the preschool years, children develop positive or negative responses about their racial status as well as that of other racial groups. Children learn about racial differences and culture from their parents and the social situations to which they are exposed. Parents are given the ominous task of helping their children understand racial perceptions and to show them that the error in thinking is with the person who displays racial antagonism (Comer, 1989, pp. 18-19).

In preparing children to deal with the issue of race and ethnic diversity, the appropriate language and concepts for describing racial diversity are important. The words, terms, phrases, and expressions that children hear others use help to form their perceptions and views about racial groups. Even though parents, adults, and helping professionals may struggle with using appropriate language in addressing racial differences (Brill, 1995), parents have the responsibility of defining what is appropriate and acceptable behavior in this domain for their children.

Unfortunately, children too frequently encounter negative language about race and ethnicity that is then incorporated into their vocabulary. This leads to misperceptions and stereotypes concerning racial groups that ultimately lay the foundation for racial discrimination.

In July 1995, President Clinton recommended to Congress and our country the reestablishment of formal relationships with Vietnam. This, of course, triggered negative reactions from many Americans. Memories and emotions associated with an undeclared war, an impoverished and war-ridden Asian country, and loss of human life were rekindled. Regardless of one's position concerning the normalization of relationships with Vietnam, the president's declaration prompted public discourse and discussion focusing on America's history, Vietnam, and the Vietnamese people.

How would you react if a relative, friend, or neighbor were to make a negative remark about a person of another ethnic origin or race in the presence of your preschooler? To make no response would connote acceptance. An intellectual discussion of racism with the preschooler would serve little purpose. Parents routinely are placed in circumstances where they need to determine the best way to mediate negative and potentially destructive social experiences for their children.

Imagine how Dennis the Menace or the Mitchells would have reacted to the aforementioned racial situation. Do you recall Dennis ever having any friends or acquaintances who were persons of color?

In a highly mobile and multicultural America, children will eventually interact with people representing diverse racial and ethnic backgrounds. What happens when children lack prior exposure to diverse populations? What obligations do parents have, even in isolated geographical areas, to teach their children about modern race relations, economic oppression, and lifestyle differences?

While research by Demo and Hughes (1990) supports the basic premise that parents are important in providing race-related socialization to their children and that race-related messages are associated with racial identity, we should consider other potentially relevant factors. As an example, Sanders Thompson suggests that, for African-American children, racial socialization messages from adult family members other than parents were more numerous and had a stronger impact on racial identification than did parental messages (1994, p. 185). In considering the African-American family structure as an extended system, the actions, comments, and demeanor of nonparental adults in the household on the development of racial attitudes and identity appear particularly germane.

Helping Families Raise Healthy Children

A major focus of this chapter has been on the function of parents and family as agents of socialization for preschoolers. When social workers and teachers hear racial epithets or contemptuous remarks from preschoolers, it is important to examine the home environment. Parents serve as a vital bond for disseminating community and societal values influencing a child's development of self.

As suggested in Chapter 2, attitudes and orientations by parents and family can be assisted by social legislation and well-organized social programs (e.g., the Family Preservation Act and Head Start). Data collected over the last 25 years clearly demonstrate "the economic value in preventing children's problems through investment early in their lives" (Scales and Brunk, 1990, p. 24). Various task forces "have showed us that programs like Head Start and good parental care really worked, and that they deserved significantly more investment than heretofore given" (Scales and Brunk, 1990, p. 24).

Secretary of Health and Human Services Donna E. Shalala, responding to a report from the Advisory Committee on Head Start Quality and Expansion, remarked, "Nothing is more important than helping parents develop child-rearing skills that keep families together and help children grow up happy" (Shalala, 1994, p. 6). Although Head Start has been lauded as a highly successful program for improving the lives of many low-income children and their families, it also faces the challenge of becoming better equipped to serve the growing and diverse needs of American families of the later 1990s. At a macro level, such expansion needs to include a broad social agenda, placing greater emphasis on race relations in curriculum and service delivery.

For the twenty-first century, Head Start policy makers have begun planning to implement more comprehensive family services and to seek new ways to provide high-quality early childhood experiences. As one priority, Head Start leadership is considering full day/full year programs and seeking mechanisms to better target and serve families with younger children. The Head Start Advisory Committee hopes to build on the identified strengths of the program, parental involvement, and community orientation (Advisory Committee, 1994).

CASE EXAMPLE

Keith Romero is a social worker in the family life education division of a three-county community action agency in rural northern California. A 44-year-old Hispanic American, Keith resides within the area. During the four years he has been employed by the agency, his primary role has been to lead parent effectiveness groups and to function as a liaison to the Head Start program, which is also a member of the county community action agency.

Referrals for Keith's groups routinely originate from Children's Services, the Head Start program, the local community mental health system, and various family service associations. Because of limited resources in the rural counties served, the referring agencies have formed an interagency cluster group to address common needs and concerns of children and families. Keith is an active member of this organization.

Prior to establishing a parenting group, Keith receives a social history of each parent interested in participating. Keith has worked closely with each of the referring agencies to construct a comprehensive assessment instrument that includes presenting problems as well as providing a detailed background of family and parent needs and resources. Following a review of the social history, Keith interviews a prospective parent to judge suitability for participation in a particular group.

Frequently parents seek admission into Keith's groups to deal with acting-out behaviors exhibited by their children. A typical scenario presents a child in trouble at home or at school, already involved with the court system. The parents are encouraged to seek and participate in individual and/or family intervention. Referrals to the parenting group frequently come via the school or courts.

Keith reviewed the application and social history of Carlos and Jean Lopez requesting enrollment in a group for couples with preschoolers entitled "Enrichment and Boundaries for Our Youngsters." Carlos and Jean have been married for five years and have one son, four-year-old Billy. Carlos is 41 years of age, Hispanic American, and a supervisor of work crews at a nearby winery. Jean is a 34-year-old white who works second shift as a nursing assistant at the local community hospital.

Billy's unacceptable language and defiance of authority caused Carlos and Jean to seek professional help at a child guidance clinic. Recently, when Jean told Billy to go to bed prior to the end of his favorite television show, *The Simpsons*, Billy replied "This is bullshit!" and stomped up the stairs. Carlos and Jean were stunned. Several similar instances of negative behavior at home and with friends led to the request to join a parenting group.

Following a careful review of the social history and an interview with Carlos and Jean, Keith found that because of the parents' employment schedules Billy was with his mother during the day and with his dad in the evenings. While this arrangement eliminated day care, Billy's time was highly organized during the daytime with his mother but highly unstructured in the evenings with his dad.

Once or twice a week, Billy accompanied Carlos to a local bar and grill to eat dinner, where they associated with winery employees after work. The atmosphere at the bar and grill was typical of an adult sports bar, with the game of the week being shown on large-screen television monitors. Carlos looked forward to time at the bar and grill as a reward for hard work at the winery and at home. The language is usually coarse; people at the bar seldom realized that Billy was present.

During the other weeknights, Billy typically stayed home with his father and watched television. Carlos sometimes joined his son but many times was busy around the house preparing dinner, doing minor repairs on the home, and completing domestic duties. Carlos seldom monitored Billy's television viewing.

As a social worker, Keith saw marital and family dynamics and issues that require attention. He decided that Carlos and Jean are appropriate for an educational group focusing on child enrichment and boundary setting. Comments by Carlos and Jean during their interview suggest they were motivated, interested in topics regarding child rearing, and would be an asset to the group. Carlos and Jean signed release-of-information forms allowing Keith and the referring family service social worker to communicate and monitor their progress.

Keith's groups usually explore parenting issues related to dual-income families, monitoring of television, enrichment activities, role modeling, parental coalitions, the influence of others, and appropriate boundary setting. In addition, a racial and ethnic diversity represented in the group's membership could yield opportunities to discuss the development of healthy attitudes toward self and others as well as other topics related to race.

TIME TO THINK!

While this chapter's case example features a social worker engaged in group work, Keith is also highly involved in community organization, especially the coordination and delivery of family preservation services. How will the consideration of macro-level influences enhance the effectiveness of group work practice? In what ways could Keith's group be seen as a microcosm of society? How effective is group work as an agent of socialization for parents? What community-level problems do you see in Keith's agency? What contradictory tendencies are apparent here?

MACRO SYSTEMS AND THE LOPEZ FAMILY

In this chapter we have stressed the importance of parental figures in the socialization of preschoolers. Billy, like most children, looks to his parents for guidance and as models for behavior. With Billy's well-being and family preservation in mind, consider relevant organizational, community, societal, and global elements.

Organizational Level

The Lopez family is fortunate that the rural area in which they live has a well-integrated network of social service organizations. The presence of a professional cluster group concentrating on family issues demonstrates both organizational and community commitment to family preservation. Such groups are small, voluntary, and formed around a common concern. They may or may not establish a plan of action and may be leaderless.

By taking part in the cluster group, Keith and other social workers become familiar with both family needs and resources. While Billy does not currently attend a preschool or day care program, his parents may want to consider the merits of enrolling Billy in a preschool with an educational emphasis.

Through knowing the focus of programming at various preschool and day care programs, social workers can better assist clients like the Lopez family. By nurturing close relationships with various preschool programs, social workers encourage preschools and Head Start programs to better address community needs.

While Keith lives in the community in which he practices, one might wonder if he is familiar with wineries or hospitals as workplaces. As a supervisor of winery workers, Carlos associates and socializes with field and manual laborers. In his business, the supervisor is a friend and a confidant. Winery workers not only work together but drink together. Their language is direct and often coarse.

Conversely, the hospital where Jean works is a very structured environment. Physicians, nurses, and nursing aids have well-defined roles and a planned regimen. Jean clocks in at 4 P.M. and clocks out at midnight five days a week. She rarely sees her colleagues outside of work and spends most of her daytime hours working at home and participating in planned activities with Billy. Billy experiences two very different parenting styles each workday. Interestingly, Carlos and Jean's parenting methods reflect the interaction styles at their respective workplaces.

Community Level

Carlos and Jean live in a rural community in northern California, near Napa Valley. The people who live and work in this area come from many different backgrounds and are of various nationalities. While interracial marriage is not uncommon in the region, Billy has been confronted by some neighborhood children about being biracial. Billy has other buddies his age in the neighborhood who are also biracial, including Ricky, his best friend. This seems to be reassuring to both Billy and his parents.

Generally, members of this northern California area are hard-working and trustworthy people. Much like farmers of the Midwest, they believe in what Martinez-Brawley and Blundall (1991, p. 315) call "a fair and just world," where people take responsibility for themselves. Only when forces are deemed outside of a victim's control is help acceptable. Having this cultural insight, one might argue that Carlos and Jean are clearly exceptions to the rule. Why did these parents seek help for Billy? Keith's experiences working in this geographical area concur with findings from research conducted by Martinez-Brawley and Blundall (1991, p. 318). They suggest that young children in farm areas are more likely to be seen as helpless; therefore services for children are more acceptable and less stigmatizing. So, it is acceptable for Carlos and Jean to seek help for Billy's acting out behavior. Meanwhile, Keith and the other professionals in the cluster group assess and seek new ways to encourage families of children-at-risk to come forward for help.

Keith finds the lack of community resources to be a major problem in group work. While the integration of social service programs and the presence of preschool and day care programs have already been highlighted as important factors, parents in Keith's groups frequently voice concerns related to the need for playgrounds, parks, pools, and community life for their children.

As a result, Keith has allocated an increasing portion of his time to community planning and projects aimed at enhancing local recreational opportunities and cultural life for families and youth. In the beginning, Keith felt hesitant to use agency time to attend these meetings and to serve on the Regional Recreation Board. But Keith knows that many of his clients need affordable and family-centered activities and programs in the community to assist in building and maintaining quality family relationships. He has the support of his supervisor in developing these broader affiliations.

Societal Level

As a social worker and lifelong resident of the state of California, Keith is keenly aware of the impact that changes in state or national priorities can bring to human services. When Ronald Reagan was governor, social services in Keith's community received low priority or were discontinued. Indeed, not until the last five years has the family life education division been able to offer group intervention to parents. While privatization of services and cutbacks have curtailed service delivery, the impetus for Keith's family life education group work was grounded in the perception of higher productivity and cost effectiveness (Motenko et al., 1995).

Like Carlos and Jean, several other people in the groups have expressed concerns over the influence of television and video games on children. In the rural area where Keith practices, people who cannot receive cable television acquire satellite dishes with a myriad of channels. Television is a vivid connection to the outside world. Rural as well as urban children are bombarded daily with its images.

Familiar with research on this subject, Keith is interested in assessing the impact of television on children in rural areas and in his community in particular. Toward this end, Keith started discussing research possibilities and potential funding sources with his supervisor and a colleague at the agency. Since rural residents tend to be more physically and socially isolated, Keith is interested in examining parental control over both the amount of television and the content of programs watched by younger children.

He is also considering forming a group of parents interested in exploring and discussing the impact of television on children in the community. Several people in Keith's groups saw the issue as an opportunity to explore policies aimed at regulating television programming for children.

International Level

The Lopez family lives in "wine country." The international marketplace for wine and wine products has a direct bearing on this, the biggest industry in the valley. Both social workers and clients realize that if the wine industry were to suffer a setback, there would be widespread ramifications for the local economy and residents.

As an example, each year new investors from around the world enter vineyard ownership in the valley. What has been traditionally a family owned and managed industry has gradually become an international venture. Foreign investors see the wine industry as chic and trendy. But with each new owner come new policies and employment turnover.

Typical of California, the members of this community represent a wide array of nationalities. Migrants from Mexico make up much of the population of this region. For Keith and other social workers, this means becoming acquainted with customs and values that have their origin in other lands. Attitudes and behaviors of clients can often be connected to practices derived from other countries. Social workers are continually educating themselves to the meaning of human behavior from a cultural perspective.

Keith is aware, for example, that in Hispanic American families the father is often the decision maker and disciplinarian (Lum, 1992, p. 179). And while commitment by Carlos to the helping process is crucial for Billy's sake, Carlos also serves as an example to other Hispanic American males that engaging in formalized helping is acceptable.

Finally, tourism is a factor to be considered. Northern California ranks as one of the most popular destinations for travel internationally. Each year, many tourists pass through this three-county area on their vacation travels, and wineries and other local businesses and jurisdictions rely on revenues generated by tourists.

APPLYING A SOCIAL WORK FRAMEWORK: SYMBOLIC INTERACTION

In our case example, we begin to see how one child's identity is being shaped through human interaction. Billy's father and mother, the workers at the bar and grill, his neighborhood friends, and television each have an influence in shaping Billy's language, sense of self, and perspective on right and wrong.

A warning bell sounded for Carlos and Jean concerning Billy's development. Fortunately, they answered the call by seeking professional help. Through participation in Keith's group, Billy's parents learned new techniques aimed at monitoring and controlling input from others in Billy's life. In group intervention, Carlos and Jean gained insight into role-modeling for their son. The group assisted Carlos and Jean in becoming aware of and reflecting upon their parenting styles and the type of experiences most beneficial for Billy.

Thus, Carlos has reevaluated the wisdom of exposing Billy to the neighborhood bar and grill as well as to the company of other wine workers. It is clear that Billy's language echoes what he has heard, whether from acquaintances or television. Also, parents must decide what their preschool child should see on television. If, as symbolic interactionists believe, children develop a sense of self through social comparison and the appraisals of others, Jean and Carlos must decide who they want to serve as role models for Billy.

Billy is fortunate that he has two parents unified in their commitment to do whatever is best for him, in seeking professional assistance, and in examining their parenting goals and methods. Strong parental cooperation in the helping process is an invaluable asset.

With regard to macro-level social work, Keith is using group work to assess community needs and priorities. He knows that the availability of preschools, recreational facilities, forums for discussing race relations, family preservation services, and the impact of television are powerful influences affecting preschoolers in his community. As a result, Keith is active in the multi-agency cluster group and works with professional colleagues in research and policy analysis aimed at assessing these important issues.

————————— **SUGGESTED ACTIVITIES** —————————

1. Reserve a Saturday morning for watching cartoons on television. Identify products being marketed in programming and commercials. Give special attention to the depiction of women and men, of girls and boys. What messages are being transmitted to young children?

2. Ask friends and acquaintances about day care centers in your neighborhood. Ask them to rank the top three day care providers, listing the strengths of each.

3. Practice being an active listener to racial phrases, statements, and jokes that have negative connotations. Were children present when you heard these comments being made? Discuss with a classmate of a race other than your own how these comments might influence children and their perceptions of racial minorities.

-------------------- REFERENCES --------------------

Advisory Committee (1994). Executive Summary: The Report of the Advisory Committee on Head Start Quality and Expansion. *Children Today*, 22(4), 5-41.

Blankenhorn, D. (1995). Life Without Father. *USA Weekend*, February 24-26, 6-7.

Brill, N. (1995). *Working with People*. White Plains, NY: Longman.

Clarke-Stewart, K., Gruber, C., & Fitzgerald, L. (1994). *Children at Home and in Day Care*. Hillsdale, NJ: Lawrence Erlbaum Associates, Publishers.

Comer, J. (1989). Racism and the Education of Young Children. In F. Rust & L. Williams (Eds.), *The Care and Education of Young Children*. New York: Teachers College Press.

Cooley, C. (1909). *Social Organization*. New York: Scribner's.

Demo, D., & Hughes, M. (1990). Socialization and Racial Identity Among Black Americans. *Social Psychology Quarterly*, 53(3), 364-374.

Deutsch, F. (1983). *Child Services on Behalf of Children*. Monterey, CA: Brooks/Cole Publishing Company.

Edelman, M. (1989). Economic Issues Related to Child Care and Early Childhood Education. In F. Rust & L. Williams (Eds.), *The Care and Education of Young Children*. New York: Teachers College Press.

Feld, S., & Radin, N. (1982). *Social Psychology for Social Work and the Mental Health Professions*. New York: Columbia University Press.

Halpern, R. (1995). Children on the Edge: An Essay Review. *Social Service Review*, 69(1), 131-151.

Hashima, P., & Amato, P. (1994). Poverty, Social Support, and Parental Behavior. *Child Development*, 65(2), 394-403.

Homans, G. (1950). *The Human Group*. New York: Harcourt Brace Jovanovich, Inc.

Kline, S. (1993). *Out of the Garden*. New York: Verso.

Lazar, B. (1994). Under the Influence: An Analysis of Children's Television Regulation. *Social Work*, 39(1), 67-74.

Lum, D. (1992). *Social Work Practice and People of Color*. Pacific Grove, CA: Brooks/Cole Publishing Company.

Lum, D. (1995). Cultural Values and Minority People of Color. *Journal of Sociology and Social Welfare*, 12(1), 59–74.

Martinez-Brawley, E., & Blundall, J. (1991). Whom Shall We Help? Farm Families' Beliefs and Attitudes about Need and Services. *Social Work*, 36(4), 315–321.

Mc Hale, S., Crouter, A., Mc Guire, S., & Updegraff, K. (1995). Congruence between Mothers' and Fathers' Differential Treatment of Siblings: Links with Family Relations and Children's Well-Being. *Child Development*, 66(1), 116–128.

Mead, G. (1934). *Mind, Self, and Society*. New York: Doubleday.

Motenko, A., et al. (1995). Privatization and Cutbacks: Social Work and Client Impressions of Service Delivery in Massachusetts. *Social Work*, 40(4), 456–463.

Nielsen Media Research (1990). *Report on Television*. Northbrook, IL: Nielsen Company.

Palmer, E. (1988). *Television and America's Children*. New York: Oxford University Press.

Phillips, D., & Whitebook, M. (1990). The Child Care Provider: Pivotal Player in the Child's World. In S. Chehrazi (Ed.), *Psychosocial Issues in Day Care*. Washington, DC: American Psychiatric Press, Inc.

Rowe, P. (1992). Child Abuse Telecast Floods National Hotline. *Children Today*, 21(2), 11.

Sanders Thompson, V. (1994). Socialization to Race and Its Relationship to Racial Identification Among African Americans. *Journal of Black Psychology*, 20(2), 175–188.

Scales, P., & Brunk, B. (1990). Keeping Children on Top of the States' Policy Agendas. *Child Welfare*, 69(1), 23–32.

Schneider, C. (1987). *Children's Television*. Chicago: NTC Business Books.

Shalala, D. (1994). Remarks by Donna E. Shalala. *Children Today*, 22(4), 6.

Slayton, A. (1993). First Things First: Paternity and Child Support for Nonmarital Children. *Children Today*, 22(1), 22–24.

Thyssen, S. (1995). Care for Children in Day Care Centers. *Child and Youth Care Forum*, 24(2), 91–106.

Tischler, H. (1990). *Introduction to Sociology*. New York: Holt, Rinehart and Winston, Inc.

Turner, J. (1974). *The Structure of Sociological Theory.* Homewood, IL: The Dorsey Press.

U.S. Department of Commerce (1995). *Statistical Abstract of the United States.* Lanham, MD, p. 57.

Van Evra, J. (1990). *Television and Child Development.* Hillsdale, NJ: Lawrence Erlbaum Associates, Publishers.

Whitebook, M., Howes, C., & Phillips, D. (1990). *Who Cares? Child Care Teachers and the Quality of Care in America.* Final Report. National Child Care Staffing Study. Oakland, CA: Child Care Employee Project.

Zigler, E., & Lang, M. (1991). *Child Care Choices.* New York: The Free Press.

CHAPTER

4

Children of School Age

In the mid-1980s, Ryan White, a 13-year-old student from Kokomo, Indiana, who had been diagnosed with AIDS, captured the attention of a nation. His efforts to stay in school and to inform a fearful public about AIDS were not his first crusades. Having been diagnosed with hemophilia soon after birth, Ryan depicts his life as "growing up different," in *Ryan White: My Own Story:*

> Most hemophiliacs look like me—small and skinny with knobby knees and elbows from all the times our joints got swollen from bleeds. Me, I look at myself in the mirror and figure, small but tough. But I guess a lot of people, my grandparents included, think we hemophiliacs don't look like we're built to last. Before Factor VIII, we didn't. Doctors told Mom that a severe hemophiliac like me could only expect to live maybe to age fourteen or fifteen. In between, he'd spend a lot of time being rushed to the emergency room whenever he got a bump or a scrape. (1991, p. 16)

A contaminated batch of Factor, the blood-clotting agent designed to save the lives of hemophiliacs, infected Ryan with AIDS. Even though Ryan frequently experienced prejudicial treatment as a result of hemophilia, his greatest challenges came from discrimination as a result of AIDS.

Ryan White shared a universal desire of school-age children. In *People Weekly's* cover story, Ryan stated, "All I wanted was to go to school and fit in" (Friedman, 1988, p. 89). "Fitting in" for a 13-year-old hemophiliac with AIDS was not an easy task in Kokomo, Indiana. Instead, "Because Ryan's diagnosis was one of the first in Indiana, fear and panic among parents caused a battle in the school district [that] split the community." Ryan's mother, Jeanne, added "They didn't know what to do about AIDS. They didn't want it involved in their lives" (SerVaas, 1988, p. 54).

Western school administrators cited a lack of policy and guidelines from the State Board of Health as the reason they denied Ryan the right to attend school. The possibility of infection of other children became an emotional flashpoint. With encouragement and support from his mother, Ryan became the first student in the United States to protest being barred from school as a result of AIDS.

Jeanne White immediately took Ryan's case to court. The Whites argued that the Western school system's actions constituted discrimination against a handicapped child. Unfortunately, the court system responded with bureaucratic delay. Meanwhile, summer break was nearing an end and fall classes were about to begin at Western.

On the day he became a seventh-grader, Ryan participated in school by using a two-way phone hookup between home and classroom. Since the likelihood of Ryan attending school was bleak, Jeanne felt that if the school was willing to offer this arrangement, they should try it. Ryan responded, "I don't want to be treated worse than other kids, but I don't want to be treated better either. I just wanted to be the same…. It stinks…. I wanted to say, it sucks" (White and Cunningham, 1991, pp. 82–83).

As time passed, a Howard County health official and an expert from the Indiana State Board of Health agreed that Ryan's condition was not a threat to other students and that he belonged in school. Although the Western school system appeared unyielding, pressure from media reports and the refusal of Western's appeal by the state of Indiana cleared the way for Ryan's eventual return to school. A separate water fountain and a private toilet were included in the numerous conditions of his attendance.

Upon reentering school, Ryan was met by protest from a concerned citizens group, the removal of over 20 children from junior high, and a spirit of social isolation. Ryan soon learned that being at school could be almost as lonely as being at home. After a bullet was fired into the White home, Ryan and his family relocated to Cicero, Indiana, and a more understanding and friendly school environment.

Ryan White's story is offered both as testimony to the courage of this young man and as an example of how students with special needs are confronted by discriminatory acts within school systems. Ryan became a casualty of AIDS through hemophilia, but many children with other forms of physical, learning, and developmental disabilities routinely encounter insensitive and ill-informed educational, legal, and social systems. As we look at macro systems affecting elementary school children, let Ryan White's story serve as a reminder that social acceptance is a prerequisite for learning. An enhanced educational environment requires a climate in which children will be treated equally in every possible way.

THEORY: NORMALIZATION

"Social work is more than a science, because the profession is value oriented" (Kilty and Meenaghan, 1995, p. 445). Social work operates under an inherently political context. As social workers contemplate the use of various theoretical orientations for research and practice, larger societal forces such as political conservatism have "pushed for a testing of interventions and theories" (Kilty and Meenaghan, 1995, p. 445). The micro aspects of social work have resulted in a proliferation of theories and research addressing the effectiveness of individual and family interventions, instead of efforts directed toward the definition of problems and conditions afflicting different groups of people in our society.

By way of avoiding the "micro trap" that characterized the 1980s and 1990s, the macro concept of normalization provides a broader thesis. First written in 1959 into Danish law for regulating services for the mentally retarded, **normalization** can be defined as promoting an existence for clients as close to normal as possible (Bank-Mikkelsen, 1969). Wolfensberger describes normalization in human services as providing clients access to culturally valued behaviors and activities and suggests, "in as many aspects of a person's functioning as possible, the human manager will aspire to elicit and maintain behaviors and appearances that come as close to being normative as circumstances and the person's behavioral potential permit" (1972, p. 28). "Normative" is defined in relationship to typical or conventional actions.

Some people believe normalization is more value judgment than theory. Normalization in our view is helpful in conceptualizing research questions and macro-level assessment in social work practice. Wolfensberger warns:

> The normalization principle as stated is deceptively simple. Many individuals will agree to it wholeheartedly while lacking awareness of even the most immediate and major corollaries and implications. Indeed, many human managers endorse the principle readily while engaging in practices quite opposed to it—without being aware of this discordance until the implications are spelled out. (1972, p. 29)

The Applicability of Normalization for Different System Levels

Normalization is an analytical principle applicable for assessment and change with individuals, families, schools, work settings, service agencies, and neighborhoods, as well as laws and the government (Wolfensberger, 1972). Normalization maximizes **mainstreaming**, as it advocates keeping the client in the larger group. The converse of mainstreaming is **segregated service** in special classes, whereby persons with similar disabilities are segregated.

Following the logic of normalization, clients achieve integration when they experience culturally valued lives. Residence in a normal community, age-appropriate types of social interaction, and typical utilization of community resources are examples of normative participation. Availability of public transportation, places of worship, hospitals, schools, stores, recreational facilities, and job placements are essential. "Integration is only meaningful if it is social integration; i.e., if it involves social interaction and acceptance, and not merely physical presence" (Wolfensberger, 1972, p. 48).

Physical Integration

Programs and services for physical integration should be community based and "absorbed into the prevailing social, economic, educational, etc. systems," not isolated or segregated within an organization or community (Wolfensberger, 1972, p. 48). Services should also be physically and socially accessible to clients, including being in close proximity to transportation routes and systems.

In many respects, physical integration involves a complete package. For example, one could centrally locate social service programs in the county courthouse, near other services, businesses, and transportation routes, but relegate social services to the basement, with inconvenient and inferior office facilities. Or, consider administrative decisions at schools that squeeze social work, tutoring, and educational enrichment programs into former janitor rooms or storage spaces. In each of these cases, clients are physically part of the mainstream but are still perceived as different and inferior.

Social Integration

Beyond physical integration, social workers are especially interested in assessing the social integration of services and programs. Social integration is affected by how both clients and others perceive the actual services and facilities. Labels, language, and symbols associated with persons, sites, and facilities are important in promoting culturally valued social programs and in building a desired perception of social services.

As mentioned earlier, a goal of social work intervention is to build a positive image for client services. Consider, for example, your reaction when you see a smaller than normal yellow school bus. Do you look at this type of bus differently? Why? Could it be because you know that students with developmental disabilities use this kind of bus?

Similarly, imagine the keen disappointment when students find out that they have been placed in Level 3 classes, while their friends are in Level 1 or 2 classes. They receive a clear message about academic status and promise.

Enhancing Social Images and Personal Competencies

In subsequent publications, Wolfensberger (1983) proposes that professionals should work to promote socially valued roles and to improve life conditions for clients. He suggests an emphasis on the strengthening of clients' social images, or their perceived value in the eyes of others, and enhancement of their competencies.

> In our society, image enhancement and competency enhancement can be assumed to be generally reciprocally reinforcing, both positively and negatively. That is, a person who is competency-impaired is highly at risk of becoming seen and interpreted as of low value, thus suffering image-impairment; a person who is impaired in social image is apt to be responded to by others in ways that impair/reduce his/her competency. Both processes work equally in the reverse direction; that is a person whose social image is positively valued is apt to be provided with experiences, expectancies, and other life conditions which generally will also increase his/her competencies, and a person who is highly competent is also more apt to be imaged positively. (Wolfensberger, 1983, p. 236)

Thus, whether through physical setting, the use of language and symbols, activities and programming, relationships, or the groupings of clients, social workers should approach helping from the standpoint of valuing persons in both word and action. Following the principles of normalization, if fifth-graders at a particular school typically go to football games on Friday nights, sit in a certain section of bleachers at home games, and wear school colors, then participation by clients in this type of culturally valued event should be supported.

A caveat: As social work students you may not be familiar with normalization as a fundamental educational theory. Yet it may present a more appropriate basic framework for considering macro issues than other orientations presented in the social work literature. Kilty and Meenaghan's (1995) proposition appears worthy of consideration. They submit that the conceptualization of social work problems and process is influenced by the current sociopolitical context. The relative obscurity of normalization might best be explained by its incongruence with the individual-responsibility political agenda during the past two decades.

DEVELOPMENTAL ISSUES

Several aspects of human development for children between the ages of six and eleven are examined in this chapter. Psychological, intellectual, and moral growth are dominant themes during middle childhood. Socially, a key developmental issue involves entry into formalized education. At age six, most children experience life in primary school—school buses, teachers, classrooms, classmates, and structured academic curricula.

The particular school a child attends will depend on several factors. Generally, children attend school in the geographical area in which they live. Unless they are trying to achieve racial desegregation, public school systems will typically assign students to the elementary school nearest their home. In the case of private or parochial school education, a child's acceptance is frequently contingent upon an ability to pay and the passing of screening tests.

Real estate agents often attest that among the first questions prospective home buyers ask are those regarding location and quality of schools for their children. Schools ranking high on academic achievement indicators are located in more affluent and higher-priced housing areas. Our school systems reflect a segregated society—not solely on the basis of race, but also on the basis of socioeconomic class.

During the 1960s and in the midst of landmark U.S. Supreme Court decisions ordering the end of racially segregated school systems in major cities in the United States the term *white flight* was coined. **White flight** refers to the movement of whites from city to suburban areas, often to escape racially desegregated school systems.

Suburban flight might better describe contemporary relocation patterns of residents in relationship to formalized primary and secondary education. **Suburban flight** occurs when people, regardless of race, move from cities to more affluent school districts located in the suburbs in their quest for a higher-quality education for their children. The prerequisite for suburban flight is having the money for more expensive housing.

Schools at Risk

Before addressing the issue of students at risk, let's examine the problem of schools at risk. Montgomery and Rossi (1994) suggest that some schools—with negative milieus and limited resources—put students in jeopardy as a result of the poor quality of the school environment.

Other schools provide a multitude of administrative and supportive services to complement traditional classroom experiences. Extracurricular events, counseling services, athletics, clubs, and active parent-teacher associations help provide a full and balanced school climate that permeates every aspect of the educational program and teacher-student relationships.

Unfortunately, not all schools can afford auxiliary services and activities. Indeed, "researchers increasingly conceptualize poor educational performance as the outcome of a process of **disengagement** that may begin as early as a child's entry into school" (Montgomery and Rossi, 1994, p. 12). If students do not identify with various school-sponsored programs and activities, they become at risk of poor academic performance and of dropping out.

Montgomery and Rossi further suggest that schools engage in **investment behavior**, in which school officials "encourage student involvement in academic and extracurricular activities by stimulating students' interests, increasing their personal resources, and rewarding their efforts" (1994, p. 12). The inability or unwillingness of a school district to finance education, however, often precludes investment behavior. In the case of economically disadvantaged school systems, investment types of opportunities for poor children may be very limited and supply little encouragement to students to persevere in school.

Students at Risk

According to Magrisso:

> The young child's positive growth and development are reliant upon his (her) effective movement between spheres of influence—the environments of school, home and neighborhood...the school's vision of the at-risk child is framed within an epidemiological model—one that attributes problematic characteristics to the child, and that the child brings from the home into the school. (1992, p. 26)

However, it may be more appropriate to assess students at risk by observing the relationships that exist between schools and students. Students are often first identified as being at risk by their classroom behavior and achievement. Rather than classifying the student as a problem, a more dynamic explanation involves assessment of teacher, classroom, and school expectations in relationship to student performance.

As an example, when a student who is severely visually impaired attends a school that relies heavily upon classroom lecture, note taking, and paper-pencil essay testing, why is the student at risk? In part, the student's visual impairment limits her or his note-taking and essay-writing abilities. But classroom expectations also serve to place the student at risk. If students were required to use audio recorders for note taking and all examinations were oral, a visually impaired student might even have an academic advantage.

Traditional Responses to Students at Risk

Assessing organizational response by school systems to the task of educating at-risk students reveals wide variations. The challenge for many schools is to provide a quality education for a diverse academic and socioeconomic student population. How can educational programs be designed to enhance opportunities for at-risk students without lowering the level of social acceptance and the students' ability to fit in? Unfortunately, the traditional reaction to student diversity often involves "various systems of sorting and selecting students into more homogeneous learning groups" (Legters and McDill, 1994, p. 24).

Legters and McDill (1994, pp. 24–25) provide several examples of established sorting and selecting methods used in schools. They include:

> **grouping/tracking**: Separating students into distinct academic streams—college preparation, vocational, and general.
>
> **retention**: Keeping students back as a result of failing to reach required levels of achievement.
>
> **special education**: Placing low-achieving students into special programs designated for the physically disabled and mentally challenged.
>
> **pull-out programs**: Removing students from their regular class 20 to 40 minutes per day for small-group remedial instruction. Supported by the national Chapter 1 program, the largest federal educational program for helping students at risk, the pull-out programs tend to be the most popular delivery strategy.

"In practice, however, the research evidence available suggests that these strategies add few benefits and often may do more to limit than to increase learning opportunities" (Legters and McDill, 1994, p. 25). Additionally, sorting and selecting programs by definition obstruct students' abilities to fit in, feel accepted, and maintain involvement in socially valued experiences.

Emerging Strategies for Students at Risk and Disabled Students

Biklen submits that before significant alterations are made in school programs for students with disabling conditions and at-risk students, "how we in this society think about disabilities must change, and change dramatically"(1985, p. 174). Toward this end, five broad principles important for influencing fuller integration of disabled and at-risk students in schools are identified:

Principle 1: Equity requires an institutional commitment.
In order for equity to occur for persons with disabilities, integration cannot be viewed as experimental. School systems and state departments of education must mandate and guarantee integration. For students with disabilities this means that any accommodations which facilitate learning are seen as normal by school administrators, teacher, parents and students.

Principle 2: Activism, rights, and equity, not pity, compassion, and benevolence, will foster the emergence of integration.
As a society, we must move beyond a charity mentality where students with disabilities and at-risk are pitied. A more productive approach views students having special needs with high regard and channeling energies into activities aimed at securing a quality education.

Principle 3: Normalization must become part of everyday life.
Students with disabilities and at-risk in schools need to be treated as normally as possible. This requires broad-based support in communities and nationally.

Principle 4: Working with people with disabilities is important.
Recognition and support for the value and dedication required of these staff persons should be an intrinsic part of the mission of each school district. Stereotypes and myths abound with regard to disabled students. Negative attitudes toward students with any form of disability need to be eliminated.

Principle 5: The success of integration throughout society will be determined by our commitment to it.

Consensus building that promotes the integration of students in schools is crucial. Without a general value or belief in support of integration, success will be weak and inconsistent. (Biklen, 1985, pp. 175–186)

As a social work student, you may already be assessing how avidly schools embrace Biklen's five principles. However, they are not offered as "quick fixes." Indeed, securing human rights for any group is likely to be more of a process than a product. Schultz (1992) suggests that the overall complexity of the public educational system, with over 15,000 school districts, school boards, and superintendents, itself produces a formidable force in inhibiting the reshaping of education in the United States.

On a positive note, however, Legters and McDill (1994) remind us that progress is being made in communities and school systems across our nation with regard to the education of various at-risk students. Advancements include:

1. *Changes in curriculum and testing*—As opposed to the traditional model of offering students with learning difficulties the same content at a slower pace, some schools are moving to curricula that focus on matching content with each student's interests and academic strengths. This includes coordinating means of testing with each student's aptitude for test taking. These curricula emphasize individualization within the general classroom context.

2. *Integration of academic and vocational skills*— The reenactment of the Carl D. Perkins Vocational and Applied Technology Act (Public Law 101-476) by Congress in 1990 has moved many schools to reexamine the link between vocational and academic education. Predicated on the tenet that, when students use academic materials to work on "real life" situations and tasks, students' motivation increases, various models have emerged in an attempt to inspire student learning.

3. *Use of mentoring programs*—A much publicized approach to encourage positive attitude toward schools involves the use of adult volunteers from the community as student mentors or advocates. A well-conceived mentoring program connects a wide range of student learners with volunteers who have adequate commitment and time to successfully sustain relationships with students.

4. *Creation of cooperative learning programs*—Envision students of varying abilities working together in small teams to complete a group task or goal. Typically, in this scenario, competition is encouraged between teams so that each student's efforts contribute to goal attainment. Peer pressure is shifted to enhance rather than discourage student performance.

5. *Use of technological innovations*—The use of modern-day technology holds particular promise for educating all students, including those at risk. As an example, the use of computers holds potential for not only enhancing student outcomes but for increasing motivation and self-confidence.

6. *Development of multicultural education*—Appreciation of human diversity is an important element in education at all levels. Currently, public school attention to multiculturalism appears increasingly to be focused on interpersonal relations among students, combatting discrimination, and sensitivity to providing quality education for all groups of people.

While it is encouraging that many of these school programs have made headway in serving students, progress is still erratic and slow. Additionally, if "the benchmark is the provision of high-quality services to all children with disabilities in integrated community-based programs, the answer is that there is still far to go" (Bricker, Peck, and Odom, 1993, p. 275).

Community, School, Agency, and Parent Partnerships

Creating successful collaborations among schools, agencies, and parents in communities can create exciting possibilities as schools organize to maximize their potentials. By joining forces, schools, agencies, and parents can work together to better serve and support educational programs for all children through sharing information, generating support, and combining resources (Fertman, 1993).

Winter (1994) suggests that such collaborative community projects don't have to be expensive or large-scale to be effective, but they must involve commitment, energy, and time. Winter proposes, "The beauty of these groups is that community members are developing the capacity to deal together with difficult problems that no individual parent could solve alone" (1994, p. 13). Collaboratives can be insightful in defining the problems and can serve as forums for assessing community interest and organizing community support for sociopolitical action.

Dupper (1993) points out that social workers often play significant roles in implementing and sustaining school-community collaborations. He suggests that social workers bring insights about interpersonal relationships, knowledge of community resources and leaders, and understanding of complex organizations to the school setting and thus, "are in a strategic position to develop and nurture collaborative efforts between schools, businesses, and social service agencies in local communities" (Dupper, 1993, pp. 37–38).

Membership in community-based family-school-agency collaborative projects would appear particularly relevant for school social workers. Articulating the position of the Midwest School Social Work Council, Clark states that the goals of school social work services include the need "to assist multidisciplinary team members in understanding the psychosocial and cultural experience of the child in the family and community" and "to facilitate the linkage of families and appropriate resources in the community" (1992, pp. 37–38).

Picture a crowded conference room at a school district's administrative office building. School administrators, board members, parents, teachers, representatives from city council and the county commissioners' offices, the city police chief, and social workers from various child service organizations are meeting to examine the topic of children and school absenteeism, suspension, and expulsion. Several members hold political power. Some members control community resources, and others provide important insights concerning the needs of at-risk children in school. Parents express growing anxiety and a desire to share their ideas about this problem. By working together, the collaborative hopes to better understand school absenteeism in their community and eventually to pursue viable programs and interventions concentrating on changes at the organizational, community, and societal levels.

The Primary School Scene— Social Policy and Social Change

A major thrust of macro-level change in social work practice is the identification of groups of people experiencing structural oppression and organizing clients for action to improve the social environment (Long, 1995, p. 48). Considering the school environment includes assessment and monitoring of relevant policies and procedures established by school administrators, psychologists, staff members, and teachers—especially those policies that impact students at risk. Long (1995) also stresses the importance of parental input at the policy-setting level. Only through an intimate, working knowledge of school policies and procedures as well as of various state and federal laws can clients and social workers challenge local and state school systems to better provide for the academic needs of children at risk.

Social change is often manifested by program development and/or the enactment of social legislation. Social workers must be knowledgeable about the many voluntary associations (e.g., parent-teacher associations), special interest groups (e.g., child welfare councils), and clubs (e.g., music and athletic boosters) organized around student needs. These organizations can provide valuable information and serve as sources of power in advocating and lobbying for social legislation on behalf of students.

National and State Departments of Education

School social workers are employed as consultants in at least 16 state departments of education (Clark, 1991). Social workers and professional social work organizations play critical roles in shaping statewide and national agendas for programs addressing problems of children in schools.

The participation of social workers in assessing and developing federal and state initiatives is important for several reasons. Social workers are frequently called upon to intervene with school children in need. Thus, social workers are able to provide background and information for guiding program formation and development in the educational macro systems.

Social workers are not only skilled at program development and evaluation but they excel in networking with various professional organizations. Federal and state initiatives focusing on school programming for children at risk require coordination and communication between various human service agencies, professional groups, and education departments. Social workers have the skills to facilitate the interface between practitioner and policymaker necessary for effective school-based services.

The influence of federal and state mandates for school children should not be minimized. Although school programs initiated at the state and federal level are commonly modified by school systems to meet local needs, state and/or federal support and resources often serve to prompt local action. For example, state and federal mandates often pressure communities to be more responsive to issues they are reluctant to address (Helper, 1989). National drug and sex education programs for students in middle childhood have been implemented by many local districts. Barrier-free codes have made it possible for thousands of students who are physically challenged to participate at a near-normal level. Pressure from the federal government or state can provide impetus for convincing local school systems to pursue program development in these areas.

CASE EXAMPLE

Melissa Richardson is a school social worker with Hogan City Schools, a school system in a city of 150,000 residents located in southern Illinois. She serves first- through sixth-graders at the three city elementary schools. Family assessments, case management, parent counseling, and family support are her primary service responsibilities. In addition, she is frequently asked to assist with program development, training, and evaluation. She is often an advocate for families with children having special needs and is highly involved in community programs.

For the past three years, Melissa has developed a special interest in children with attention deficit disorders (ADD). Indeed, when a student exhibits behaviors that might indicate a diagnosis of ADD, the case is referred directly to Melissa. The three major factors indicating the diagnosis of ADD involve inattention, impulsivity, and hyperactivity. Children with ADD frequently exhibit difficulty in organizing themselves for school tasks and projects. ADD and other learning disabilities are usually diagnosed during elementary school.

To her credit, Melissa's approach to working with children with ADD has included both micro-level and macro-level components. She has always thought of students with ADD as a client group, not only as individuals. Melissa has been a leader in organizing parents of children with ADD both for social support and for social action, and she is a founding member of the local ADD Council. She is perceived in the community as an expert in understanding children with ADD as well as a champion for their rights. Her assistance to teachers in devising new approaches to learning for these students is well known.

Two years ago, school officials, parents, and other area social workers, in cooperation with the local ADD Council and under Melissa's leadership, formed a collaborative planning group called Assessing Attention Deficit Disorders (ATTEND). The timing of this venture was ideal. While parents of children with ADD felt depressed about their situation, they were highly motivated to take steps to assist their children. They began to request differential diagnoses for their children labeled "behavior problems." Meanwhile, strong administrative leadership and support in the school system and community created an atmosphere of empowerment for parents of children with special needs. School and community officials openly encouraged an entrepreneurial spirit for building a collaborative approach for examining diverse issues related to ADD. Examination of the organizational context of empowerment identified these factors as crucial in supporting the emergence of ATTEND (Gutierrez, GlenMaye, and DeLois, 1995).

Two themes appeared in the first two years: a general lack of awareness and knowledge concerning ADD in the school system and community, and a general disdain for ADD programming in the school expressed by both students and parents. Students with ADD were easily identifiable through their participation in school pull-out programming. Consequently, they often felt stigmatized by other students, teachers, and staff. This information was documented and used as the basis for a grant proposal requesting funding from the Hogan County Mental Health Board.

The Hogan County Mental Health Board agreed to fund a three-year pilot project to be administered by the ATTEND collaborative. The project had three purposes: first, to educate community residents, school employees, and area professionals and present to them the most recent research and information concerning ADD; second, to fund a special interagency task force for assessing school and government policies and procedures affecting students with ADD in the Hogan City School system; and finally, to conduct a needs assessment to identify families having children diagnosed with ADD.

Melissa played an important role in securing this funding by actively facilitating parent participation in educational planning and linking families with resources in the community. Many phone calls and meetings with parents, school administrators, mental health board officials, and social workers at other agencies began the process. Her in-depth knowledge of community-based assets allowed her to strategize the plan and to network the appropriate agencies and personnel. Melissa's enthusiasm in working with children with ADD energized parents and school staff members toward action. Including a program evaluation component in the grant proposal helped to secure funding for the project.

At a time when the Hogan County Mental Health Board and the Hogan City School System faced severe financial issues, Melissa and the members of ATTEND felt fortunate to be recipients of this pilot grant. The Hogan County Mental Health Board was persuaded to act favorably upon the ATTEND grant request because of its collaborative character: community agencies and schools would be working together (Carlson, Clark, and Marx, 1993). Mental health board members viewed the ATTEND proposal as an approach that emphasized coordination of services over duplication of efforts, resulting in more effective delivery of service to children with ADD.

TIME TO THINK!

Melissa Richardson, a school social worker, was faced with a multitude of demands. She was involved in both macro and micro elements of social work practice in working with children with ADD. What conditions made macro-level assessment and intervention more appropriate for Melissa than for other social workers in practice with school children? Is there anything inherent in the role of school social worker that encourages a macro-level approach to problems?

MACRO SYSTEMS AND CHILDREN WITH ADD

The client system described in this chapter is not an individual or family. Instead, children with ADD in the Hogan City Schools and their families constitute the identified client system. As a result of the recent grant, the ATTEND collaborative's work has just begun. Acknowledging that assessment is an ongoing process, we examine this client system in terms of relevant organizational, community, societal, and international factors.

Organizational Level

The Hogan City School System, the Hogan County Mental Health Board, and other related agencies appear open, flexible, and supportive of client-interagency collaboratives. Change does not appear problematic, and a tenor of cooperation apparently prevails.

However, as the ATTEND collaborative goes about its work, continued assessment of organizational climate will be imperative. Direct involvement in school policies and programming for students with ADD could create organizational tension and turmoil within the school system. As ATTEND consults with faculty and staff and ultimately suggests policy and program changes to administrators, the organizational mood may shift. School is a vital part of a child's environment. If the collaborative project alienates the school, students could suffer the consequences. Ongoing assessment by the social worker of interrelationships among the school system and other key organizations (e.g., the funding source) is critical.

During the three years of the ATTEND organization, changes will occur. For example, as membership terms expire at the Hogan County Mental Health Board, new board members will begin service, each bringing additions to the agenda. Also, it is not unusual for directors and leaders at social service agencies and boards to be replaced. As fiscal cutbacks occur, schools and social service organizations often restructure or downsize. With modifications in parental involvement, the composition and thrust of the collaborative could drift. The school social worker will need to stay abreast of the many dynamics occurring within and among the key organizations involved in the ATTEND project.

Community Level

The city of Hogan lies in rural southern Illinois. While generally interested in the problems of schools and schoolchildren, residents of the area tend to be underinformed about school issues and frugal in their spending for school programs and student services.

To increase community understanding of learning problems related to school children, Melissa has considered publishing a community newsletter. Currently, discussions center around community acceptance of yet another newsletter, since both the Hogan City Schools and the Hogan County Mental Health Board publish quarterly publications. One alternative would be to highlight various school-age problems in the Hogan City School, ADD Council, and Mental Health Board newsletters. Those opposed to this idea cite editorial control issues and possible conflicts of interest. Another option involved purchasing cable time for educating the community about various elementary school issues.

Several ATTEND collaborative members proposed that a portion of their grant project monies be used to contract an independent consulting group to conduct research, examining the effectiveness of various newsletter and cable access options in educating the community. Previous research has demonstrated broad support citywide for various mental health, children's services, and school issues, with the exception of the affluent suburban areas of West Landon Farms and Green Meadows. Some ATTEND committee members are also interested in targeting only West Landon Farms and Green Meadows for a newsletter or "cable spots."

Despite high-profile efforts to inform, children with special needs are still viewed by many in the community as either "slow" or "retarded." Social workers and organizations like the local ADD Council remain dedicated to the cause of finding new ways to promote a "normal" existence and increased acceptance for their school-age clients.

Societal Level

As a school social worker, Melissa has had a long-standing interest in working with children with disabilities. Not, however, until she read about research on ADD being conducted and supported by the National Institute of Mental Health (NIMH) did she become excited about working with this group of children. The more she learned about ADD, the greater her appreciation for the support generated nationally by the NIMH.

When reviewing literature and research on ADD, one of Melissa's most valuable resources is a 1994 publication by the National Institutes of Health entitled *Attention Deficit Hyperactivity Disorder* (#94–3572). This booklet has been extremely helpful in assisting both parents and professionals to understand ADD, to evaluate options for getting help, and to sustain hope. This valuable resource provides information, lists books on ADD for children, teens, and adults with ADD, and furnishes parents with addresses and phone numbers for national and state support groups and organizations.

Since working with children with ADD and their families, Melissa has been encouraged by the national recognition and support given to this disorder. National entities like the Attention Deficit Information Network (Ad-In) and the ADD Warehouse have been most helpful to her in gathering current research and up-to-date information on ADD. Melissa takes hope in the fact that the 1990s have been declared by the president and Congress as the "Decade of the Brain" and that her specialty area within the practice of social work has been given a high national priority.

International Level

As a school social worker in a low-profile region of the United States, Melissa makes special efforts to keep abreast of the most recent findings in her field. To receive regular and up-to-date information about learning disabilities, ADD, and other school-age problems, Melissa is considering the purchase of a computer to be able to enter the Internet and to utilize E-mail and the World Wide Web.

Melissa's interest in computer on-line services such as **Prodigy** or **America Online** and other shared data bases as a way of learning of new developments will benefit clients. Current information technology allows for an international approach to data processing and management. Indeed, many personal computers designed for use at home or in agencies contain built-in telephone modems, faxes, and language options as part of their communication packages. With these capabilities, Melissa could readily converse with professionals around the world.

In assessing the possible use of information technology for social work practice, Melissa faces several decisions. Inasmuch as the ATTEND collaborative project has available funds, which computer technologies are best suited for the project? Given her current activities, how much time can she allocate to collecting information from around the world?

Through the literature, Melissa has followed the efforts of social workers interested in promoting an international perspective for examining mental health services. In particular, she is interested in the role of community intervention in prevention and mental health promotion in other countries (Holmes and Hokenstad, 1991). Melissa hopes that by becoming familiar with mental health service delivery systems globally, new ideas will emerge for enhancing and improving the quality of life for her clients.

APPLYING A SOCIAL WORK FRAMEWORK: NORMALIZATION

Children with ADD as well as those with other kinds of disabilities desperately want to lead normal lives. They are stigmatized by school programs and services that separate and label students with disabilities as "different."

In our case example, Melissa has been a catalyst in developing a cooperative venture to examine how school systems can better educate children with ADD. To avoid the labeling and stigmatizing of students with ADD, teachers, administrators, parents, professionals, and others involved in the educational process need to be better informed about this particular disorder. In the Hogan community example, an examination of curricula, teaching styles, school policies and programs, and administrative decision making will be conducted by the ATTEND collaborative to identify mechanisms that will assure that, as much as possible, children with ADD are afforded the same opportunities as other students.

Years of practice have left Melissa with vivid memories of the anger and disappointment of students when they are singled out by school officials for special programming. She has received phone calls from parents desperate in their search to find teachers and school programs amenable to the learning style and educational plight of their son or daughter. Melissa has seen the painful expressions on faces of students and parents when teachers and school administrators in individual educational plan (IEP) conferences have referred to students with ADD as "lacking initiative," "troublemakers," or "lazy." Melissa knows that negative attitudes and behaviors directed toward people with mental disabilities must be minimized in order to attain normalization of service delivery.

Three years ago, Melissa came to the realization that battling for the rights of students with ADD case by case, teacher by teacher, and school by school was inefficient and ineffective. Funding of the ATTEND collaborative was a milestone as it signaled an initial step in Hogan City toward acknowledging systemic responsibility and concern for the treatment of children with ADD. As the school system in Hogan City begins the task of evaluation of the delivery of their educational programs, we are reminded of the real-life struggle of Ryan White and the many hurdles to be overcome by advocates for children with special needs in schools.

SUGGESTED ACTIVITIES

1. Interview a school administrator, inquiring about programming for students with special needs. Ask about task forces and/or committees of the school district or community that address issues confronting students with disabilities and their parents. How do suspension and expulsion rules apply to emotionally impaired children? What treatment is available?

2. When in your state's capital, arrange for a visit to the department of education. Ask about pending or recent landmark legislation written to protect the rights of all students.

3. Access information from the World Wide Web using an on-line computer service. Search for literature about a problem, program, or policy involving school children—for example, discipline codes. How do these apply to emotionally impaired students? Attempt to locate an E-mail address or home page to receive additional information concerning your topic.

REFERENCES

Bank-Mikkelsen, N. (1969). A Metropolitan Area in Denmark: Copenhagen. In R. Kugel & W. Wolfensberger (Eds.), *Changing Patterns in Residential Services for the Mentally Retarded*. Washington, DC: President's Committee on Mental Retardation.

Biklen, D. (1985). *Achieving the Complete School*. New York: Teachers College Press.

Bricker, D., Peck, C., & Odom, S. (1993). Integration Campaign for the New Century. In C. Peck, S. Odom, & D. Bricker (Eds.), *Integrating Young Children with Disabilities into Community Programs*. Baltimore: Paul H. Brookes Publishing Company.

Carlson, S., Clark, J., & Marx, D. (1993). School and Community Resource Collaboration. *School Social Work Journal, 17*, 47-49.

Clark, J. (1991). On the Need for States to Employ School Social Work Consultants: A Position Statement. *School Social Work Journal, 15*, 29-31.

Clark, J. (1992). School Social Work in Early Childhood Special Education. *School Social Work Journal, 16*, 37-39.

Dupper, D. (1993). School-Community Collaboration: A Description of a Model Program Designed to Prevent School Dropouts. *School Social Work Journal, 18*, 33-39.

Fertman, C. (1993). Creating Successful Collaborations Between Schools and Community Agencies. *Children Today, 22*(2), 32-34.

Friedman, J. (1988). The Quiet Victories of Ryan White. *People Weekly, 29*(21), 88-96.

Gutierrez, L., GlenMaye, L., & DeLois, K. (1995). The Organizational Context of Empowerment Practice: Implications for Social Work Administration. *Social Work, 40*(2), 249-258.

Helper, J. (1989). Utilizing Organizational Theory to Improve the Effectiveness of Implementing Evaluation and Intervention Programs in Elementary and Secondary Schools. *School Social Work Journal, 14*, 26-35.

Holmes, T., & Hokenstad, M. (1991). Mental Health Services: An International Perspective. *Journal of Sociology and Social Welfare, 18*(2), 5-23.

Kilty, K., & Meenaghan, T. (1995). Social Work and the Convergence of Politics and Science. *Social Work*, 40(4), 445-453.

Legters, N., & McDill, E. (1994). Rising to the Challenge: Emerging Strategies for Educating Youth at Risk. In R. Rossi (Ed.), *Schools and Students at Risk*. New York: Teachers College Press.

Long, D. (1995). Attention Deficit Disorder and Case Management: Infusing Macro Social Work Practice. *Journal of Sociology and Social Welfare*, 12(2), 45-55.

Magrisso, B. (1992). A Case Study Consideration of Role in Relationship to an Identified At-Risk Child. *School Social Work Journal*, 17, 25-37.

Montgomery, A., & Rossi, R. (1994). Becoming at Risk of Failure in America's Schools. In R. Rossi (Ed.), *Schools and Students at Risk*. New York: Teachers College Press.

National Institutes of Health (1994). Attention Deficit Hyperactivity Disorder, Washington, DC: U.S. Government Printing Office.

Schultz, T. (1992). Developmentally Appropriate Practice and the Challenge of Public School Reform. In D. Stegelin (Ed.), *Early Childhood Education: Policy Ideas for the 1990s*. Norwood, NJ: Ablex Publishing Corporation.

SerVaas, C. (1988). The Happier Days for Ryan White. *Saturday Evening Post*, 260(2), 52-98.

White, R., & Cunningham, A. (1991). *Ryan White: My Own Story*. New York: Dial Books.

Winter, M. (1994). Parent Networks Strengthen Communities. *Children Today*, 23(1), 12-32.

Wolfensberger, W. (1972). *The Principle of Normalization in Human Services*. Toronto: National Institute on Mental Retardation.

Wolfensberger, W. (1983). Social Role Valorization: A Proposed New Term for the Principle of Normalization. *Mental Retardation*, 21(6), 234-239.

5

Adolescence

A teenage girl stands on a street corner wearing a baggy top, ripped jeans, and worn combat boots, and smoking a cigarette. Her long hair is spiked and green. Earrings hang from her ears and a shiny stone pierces a nostril. Numerous chains dangle from her neck. To unaware passers-by, the adolescent looks dirty, displaced, and unattached. To the teenager's peers she is the epitome of a grunge.

Across the nation, adolescent youth are involved in a movement called "grunge." Some teenagers attribute this trend to the music of the Seattle-based band Nirvana, the late Kurt Cobain, and Cobain's musician-wife Courtney Love. Others suggest that grunge is a social phenomenon evidenced by a group of adolescents who wear similar clothing, share common musical interests, and project a unified dislike for established social norms. Even though a definition may depend on which teenagers are questioned, grunge has become the lifestyle of many American youth.

"The members of Nirvana did not set out to become superstars, didn't expect to move millions of units, had no way to know that an entire generation was equally tired of being lied to—by their parents, by their government and by the

music on the radio" (Alden, 1993, p. 48). In a less philosophical manner, the movement appears to have emerged out of the artistic urges of Cobain and others to "write songs that spoke to their experience of the world and that felt good when played. Loud" (Alden, 1993, p. 48).

The result of Cobain's music is a phenomenon not unlike the 1960s British music invasion, a subculture composed primarily of teenagers expressing displeasure with the establishment through actions, dress, and music. Since Cobain's suicide, the movement has not diminished. Nirvana products and collectibles continue to be in high demand (Borzillo, 1994). Until the recent violation of network rules involving profanity, grunge enjoyed its own computer forum, named Hole (after Courtney Love's band), on America Online (*New York Times*, 1995). Meanwhile, the grunge look continues to be recognized as a legitimate trend in the world of fashion and entertainment (Lieberman, 1993).

Parents commonly view popular music with suspicion, especially when it is embraced by their teenagers who are involved in "punk" or "heavy metal" subcultures. Parental protests regarding the music their children play and the clothes they wear can be counterproductive, however, and may result in unplanned consequences of stereotyping and labeling of their sons and daughters (Rosenbaum and Prinsky, 1991, p. 528).

Research literature about the relationship between punk or heavy metal types of music and delinquency indicates there is no clear correlation. Teenagers who dress in dated clothing and listen to rebellious lyrics are not necessarily unclean, involved in drugs, or engaged in destructive behavior. But the grunge stereotype produces a social label that imposes negative attributes upon the individual.

Simmons Market Research Bureau's 1994 teenage research study suggests that adolescent boys are consistent buyers and frequent users of a variety of personal-hygiene and soap products. Kate (1995) suggests that underneath grunge fashions lurk well-scrubbed bodies on which are routinely employed a multitude of personal-care products. Further, the Simmons group found that teenage boys between the ages of 12 and 19 regularly use deodorants; over one-third took a daily shower. The survey findings suggest that many teenage boys are squeaky clean.

Some adults may be tempted to judge the contemptuous ways of teenagers harshly. Although adults once experienced their own identity struggles, they often label contemporary adolescents as deviant. This chapter examines the consequences of negative labels for the adolescent. As we explore various concepts and terms, consider "grunge, not grungy"—and what a difference the changing of a single letter can make.

THEORY: LABELING

In this chapter we are less interested in why adolescents engage in actions that may be considered deviant and more concerned with the negative effects of social definitions and sanctions as influences on self-perception. What are the consequences "when certain official 'labelers' in a society (e.g., law enforcement officials or psychiatrists)" describe an adolescent or a group of adolescents as deviant (Traub and Little, 1975, p. 159)? **Labeling theory** enables us to focus upon the impact of punitive forces on adolescents.

Howard Becker describes the process of labeling: "The deviant is one to whom the label has successfully been applied; deviant behavior is behavior that people so label." Labeling theorists stress the subjective nature of rules and societal reaction to rule-breaking behavior in defining deviance. Becker concludes "social groups create deviance by making the rules whose infraction constitutes deviance, and by applying those rules to particular people" (1963, p. 9).

Several important questions emerge as one considers the effect of labeling. What happens when adolescents violate social norms or break rules? Does societal reaction vary based on the time, place, and person as well as the social significance of the rule(s) violated? If so, who defines what is deviant? Once a label is used how difficult is it to shed the unfavorable ones such as "punk," "delinquent," "druggie," or "loser?" Do negative labels contribute to future deviant behavior for adolescents in a manner that becomes a self-fulfilling prophecy?

Lemert (1951) provides valuable insight into these questions by distinguishing between primary and secondary deviance. **Primary deviance** describes individuals whose behavior is only occasionally deviant. The term **secondary deviance** is reserved for more pervasive atypical behavior. The latter individuals may feel that they have become public outcasts.

The transition from primary deviance to secondary deviance is a significant step. When primary deviance occurs, the social ramifications for those involved are minimal. A group of high schoolers are caught vandalizing a local park following an emotional soccer victory. While they are made to pay for damages and penalized by the school, the police department and school administrators believe the actions to be a "one-time occurrence." The matter is handled privately with the teenagers and their parents.

Conversely, when adolescents, individually or as a group, are given the label of deviant, and view themselves that way, the result is often social disgrace and isolation. A group of teenage girls sitting in a car in a parking lot are busted for "getting high" on marijuana. The police prosecute all involved in the incident. The word gets out that these teenagers are "druggies" and are probably involved in hard drugs as well. Soon the teenage girls experience difficulties in developing friendships and associations with other students. Friends, teachers, and even family members maintain social distance from them. The girls soon find themselves "hanging out" and associating only with one another; they begin to perceive themselves as social misfits. They are becoming "outsiders" to the conventional world. Once labeled, can these girls shed their stigma as "druggies" and juvenile delinquents? Or will the negative sanctions and stigma applied to them be overwhelming and fuel subsequent deviant acts?

"The critical variable in the study of deviance, then, is the social audience which eventually determines whether or not any episode of behavior or any class of episodes is labeled deviant" (Becker, 1964, p.11). Becker further suggests that when community officials consider exerting control over the behavior of its members, many factors not directly related to the deviant act itself are weighed. These may include "the suspect's social class, his past record as an offender, the amount of remorse he manages to convey, and many similar concerns which take hold in the shifting moods of the community" (Becker, 1964, p. 11).

In summary, the labeling perspective is best known for shifting the focus away from the individual(s) committing certain acts to the community or societal attitudes toward the individuals. As various developmental issues for adolescence are examined, it will be important to keep in mind the effect of being labeled as deviant. Our focal point will be the reaction of others and the application of labels as related to adolescent developmental issues.

DEVELOPMENTAL ISSUES

The literature on adolescence deals with a variety of topics, including rapid physical growth and maturation, sexuality, development of self-concept and self-esteem, rebellious behavior, substance abuse, career planning, and adolescent-parent relationships. Although not necessarily more difficult than other life stages, adolescence is characterized by the teenager's need for individuation. As the adolescent matures physically, she or he searches for a sense of self, often characterized by rebellion and movement away from parental figures toward peer-group affiliation.

Examining adolescent issues from a social work perspective involves searching out social forces that contribute to individual behaviors and actions. This examination does not negate the relevance of physiological and psychological components in the lives of teenagers. Instead, by highlighting social aspects of adolescent development, social workers can focus more clearly on the influence of various social systems, trends, and movements in assessing behaviors.

We must remind ourselves that adolescents are developing persons. Even though some parents may have their moments of doubt, most adolescents survive this phase and become responsible, productive citizens. Aronson addressing the topic of "people who do crazy things" in *The Social Animal,* states:

> To my mind, it does not increase our understanding of human behavior to classify these people as psychotic. It is much more useful to try to understand the nature of the situation and the processes that were operating to produce the behavior. This leads us to Aronson's first law: "People who do crazy things are not necessarily crazy." (1972, p. 9)

Using Aronson's logic, we will focus on the social processes that can help explain the actions of adolescents, as opposed to entering into a dialogue regarding the eccentric nature of adolescent endeavors. Teenagers who do crazy things need not be crazy and should not be viewed that way. "At least one quarter of all adolescents are at high risk for engaging in dangerous behaviors that threaten their health and long-term prospects" (Carnegie Council on Adolescent Development, 1996, p. 4).

Teenage Girls

The perils of being young and female are many. Problems include dropping out of school, teenage pregnancy, substance use, and exposure to violence, particularly gang activities.

Unique to teenage girls is the threat of eating disorders. Bulimia—the urge to binge and purge—is as serious as an addiction to cocaine. Anorexia is a problem of Western civilization. Bombarded by television and magazine images of thin, popular, successful women, many girls in puberty and adolescence become obsessed with weight and shape.

> They feel confident if they are losing weight and worthless and guilty if they are not. By the time the anorexia is full-blown, family members are terrified. They try everything to make their daughters eat—pleading, threatening, reasoning and tricking. But they fail because the one thing in life that anorexic girls can control is their eating.... Their thinness has become a source of power, a badge of honor.... Anorexia is a metaphor. It is a young woman's statement that she will become what the culture asks of its women, which is that they will be thin and nonthreatening. (Pipher, 1994, pp. 174-175)

The '90s are a time of intensified pressures for young women. More divorced families, chemical addiction, casual sex, and violence against women are factors that leave them vulnerable. Adolescent girls face unique and unparalleled pressures to be beautiful and sophisticated or suffer being labeled as undesirable. "America today limits girls' development, truncates their wholeness and leaves many of them traumatized" (Pipher, 1994, p. 12).

Delinquent Behavior

Adolescents are known for their tendency to test boundaries and rules. Imposing restrictions on them may constitute an invitation for problem behavior. Then social control systems are called upon to impose sanctions to help ensure that the deviant act will not recur. Labeling theory suggests, though, that sanctions levied against teenagers may create additional deviant behaviors.

An alternative approach, **deterrence theory**, contends "the threat or actual imposition of sanctions so elevates actors' perceptions of the risk of non-normative behavior that they will choose to avoid—or at a minimum to reduce the frequency of their participation in—such conduct" (Thomas and Bishop, 1984, p. 1223). Fundamental to the deterrence orientation is a belief that individuals are rational beings with the capacity for self-determination. Thomas and Bishop report the basic tenets of deterrence theory in terms of people who are:

1. Motivated by what will serve their best interest
2. Free to choose between alternative courses of action
3. Motivated to avoid deviant actions to the extent that timely and negative sanctions are a sure consequence of such behaviors (p. 1228)

An interesting debate on the merits of labeling theory versus deterrence theory as opposite orientations for explaining the effect of social control on delinquent behavior has emerged in the past two decades (Sherman and Berk, 1984). While there is no consensus as to the merits of one approach over the other, a review of literature reveals several interesting alternatives for social workers who assess the impact of social sanctions on teens.

As an example, Horwitz and Wasserman (1979), analyzing longitudinal data with teenagers, report that the offender's motivation for committing a crime is a powerful predictor of future arrest. They also suggest that for first offenders the more severe the social reaction and social control, the higher the likelihood that adolescents will commit subsequent crimes. Research indicates that the source of negative sanctions is a primary consideration. Palamara, Cullen, and Gersten (1986) report that when police and mental health workers negatively label adolescent offenders, more deviant behaviors follow. Morash (1982) suggests that parents, peers, and adult neighbors often disagree with police impressions and reaction. A negative label placed by friends is more believable and credible than those assigned by police. These findings point to the importance of both formal and informal sources of labeling in contributing to future delinquent behavior.

Finally, other studies of adolescents provide little support for either labeling or deterrence theory.

> Our impression is that labeling theorists attribute far more significance to sanctions imposed by formal or quasi-formal agents of social control than is attributed to them by those who are sanctioned. Deterrence theorists seem even more detached from the world in which most of the rest of us live. (Thomas and Bishop, 1984, p. 1244)

Both theories, however, remain viable perspectives for analyzing juvenile delinquency. Kaplan and Johnson (1991), implementing advanced statistical procedures on data from a three-wave panel of junior high school students, demonstrated how the presence of negative sanctions can predict subsequent deviant acts, even while controlling for disposition to deviance and deviant peer associations.

For social workers, a primary dilemma involves support for or opposition to various **juvenile diversion programs**, established to shield and divert teenagers from the negative aspects associated with labeling and stigmatizing in the criminal justice system. Indeed, the overall value of juvenile diversion programs is debatable (Binder and Geis, 1984).

If one accepts the premise that teenagers who misbehave are reachable, however, diversion programs are useful, especially for young, first-time offenders. Court systems can reprimand

and punish unacceptable behaviors by teenagers while giving special attention not to brand juveniles as delinquents. The distinction is between "You did something wrong" versus "You are a bad person."

Self-Concept

As stated earlier, adolescents wrestle with the development of self. Many factors contribute to the formation of self-concept and self-esteem, including gender, age, parental relationships, school activities, and part-time work (Steitz and Owen, 1992). There is a particular social-psychological interest in the emergence of one's identity in social interaction with significant others—how appraisals from parents, teachers, and peers provide teenagers with important feedback in building self-image.

As social workers, we need to explore with our clients the consequences of being labeled as deviant. Matsueda (1992), testing a multivariate causal model, indicated that both parental appraisals and prior delinquency influence the adolescent self. When deviant behavior occurs and negative social sanctioning is coupled with parental labeling, teenagers are more likely to cognitively view themselves as rule violators (secondary deviance). For many adolescents, labeling may constitute a turning point, where self-perception as a delinquent becomes lodged into the young person's self-concept. The mix of community and parental labeling serves as an important catalyst in the adoption of deviant identities in the adolescent self.

Al-Talib and Griffin (1994) lend support to the premise that both public (community) and private (parental or peer) aspects of the labeling process serve to influence self-concept. Comparing labeled, unlabeled (participating in delinquent acts but uncaught), and nondelinquent British adolescents, Al-Talib and Griffin found "a significant difference exists between the groups in the patterns of their self-concept. Adolescents who had been labeled as delinquents had a lower self-concept than their unlabeled delinquent counterparts" (1994, p. 47). They found both labeled and unlabeled adolescents who committed delinquent acts to have lower self-concepts than those who were not delinquent.

Not all research concludes that deviant social labeling results in a lower self-concept. One study, for example, found little difference in self-esteem between a sample of adolescents labeled as deviant and a sample of normal peers. Instead, only "subjects who believed that the societal view of their group was similar to the self, who had a negative evaluation of the deviant label, had lower self-esteem" (Stager, Chassin, and Young, 1983, p. 3).

Conflict with societal norms is particularly pertinent to adolescents with strong group affiliations, for example, those labeled as grunge members. If a grunge member believes that society views grunge negatively, then self-esteem is in jeopardy. Conversely, when a teenager understands that the societal view of grunge is negative, but does not internalize this view, then self-esteem is less affected.

As we reflect on these findings, social opinion about a particular adolescent group becomes relevant. Given your knowledge of the movement, do you believe that grunge members are deviant? Do they see themselves as different, cool, radical, or deviant? Is judgement about their own image based on credible information? What are sources of feedback to group members about their public reputation? To what extent are deviant adolescents isolated from the larger society?

Social workers often serve adolescents experiencing low self-esteem. In assessing the effects of being labeled as deviant, it is also important to understand the impact of any group memberships bearing stigma. While group identity and individual identity may not be synonymous, group identity is an important social force influencing adolescent self-esteem.

Drug Use

In assessing the relationship between social control and deviant behavior, Becker considered marijuana use.

In complex societies, the process can be quite complicated since breakdowns in social control are often the consequence of becoming a participant in a group whose own culture and social controls operate at cross-purposes to those of the larger society. Important factors in the genesis of deviant behavior, then, may be sought in the processes by which people are emancipated from the controls of society and become responsive to those of a smaller group. (Becker, 1963, pp. 59–60)

In 1963, marijuana use was punishable by severe penalties. It was considered dangerous to physical and mental health, and arrest and imprisonment were legal penalties.

Becker suggests that the career of a drug user can be divided into three stages: beginner, occasional user, and regular user. Crucial in problem definition is the impression by family, friends, or employer that a person is a regular marijuana user. At this point, others believe the regular user to be "irresponsible and powerless to control his own behavior, perhaps even insane. They may punish him with various kinds of informal but highly effective sanctions, such as ostracism or withdrawal of affection" (Becker, 1963, p. 61). The labeling process can be instrumental in shifting the alliance of drug users from acceptance of negative social controls of the larger society to the welcoming arms of a drug-related subculture.

A common developmental phase of adolescents often involves experimentation, use, and/or abuse of drugs. "In general, the profile of abusers suggests that they are individuals who spend a lot of time involved in drug/alcohol-related activities with friends...adolescents who abuse drugs tend to associate more with drug-using peers" (Shilts, 1991, p. 615).

Adolescent drug use, however, is a function not only of peer association: labeling and self-rejection also need to be considered. Kaplan and Fukurai (1992, p. 292), for example, tested a research model emphasizing the mediating influence of peer-group affiliation and the level of self-rejection when examining the impact of social sanctions on drug use. Their results suggest that negative social sanctioning has a direct effect on deviant peers and self-rejection: both predict drug use.

To summarize, negative social sanctions can have both direct and indirect (through self-rejection and peer-group affiliations) effects on adolescent drug use/abuse. Findings in this area further support labeling theory's implication that punishment may increase the tendency of teenagers to commit deviant actions, including the abuse of drugs.

As social workers, we are left to question the wisdom of national and state policies emphasizing punishment and incarceration of drug users. What are the ramifications of the current expansion of jail space to detain and punish those who use illegal drugs? What are the real differences between illegal and legal drug use? Are the terms "delinquent" and "criminal" reserved only for certain people and certain drugs? Is the real issue drug use or social control? How different is the labeling process for teenagers of affluent families caught with illegal substances from that of less advantaged teens?

Adolescent Gangs

Contrary to popular belief, the study of gang membership and influence in America is not a new phenomenon. Decades ago, Thrasher (1967) pioneered the study of gang life in Chicago.

In recent years, worldwide attention has been riveted on street gangs, their existence, and social significance. The defacing of public facilities with graffiti, turf battles, and increasing urban violence have focused public consciousness on gang life in America. The frequent occurrence of drive-by shootings has forced even the most detached citizen to become more concerned about gangs.

Because gang life has a street existence, the study of gangs is a complicated, dangerous endeavor, even for the most astute researcher. Primary collection of data about gangs requires intense preparation as well as advanced knowledge about group processes, structure, and cohesiveness. Although gangs are an important social problem, assessing gang life can be a hazardous undertaking.

This section relies heavily on the research of Malcolm Klein in his recent book *The American Street Gang.* We find his work on this controversial topic forthright, fair, and comprehensive. In his direct and candid style, Klein openly criticizes traditional gang intervention approaches.

Most social science literature indicates that increasing group cohesiveness also increases group morale and productivity. One of the products of gangs is crime. Most gang intervention programs, upon analysis, can be shown (have been shown, can be inferred to show) [to cause] an increase in gang cohesiveness. The obvious implication is that most gang intervention programs, without meaning to, have the net effect of increasing gang crime.... This is a warning to social workers and cops alike and to those public officials who allow, support, and encourage their anti-gang policies and programs. Anti-gang activities may inadvertently promote gang crime and violence. (1995, pp. 7–8)*

There is little consensus on the definition of a gang. Morash (1983), for example, uses the term "ganglike" with respect to youth groups to achieve objectivity and avoid any reference to delinquency in defining a gang.

Many scholars refute the notion that gangs are "criminally inclined." Gang life is viewed more as sleeping, eating, and hanging out together. Even commonly accepted athletic and church youth groups would be included in such a definition. On the other hand, delinquent acts of gang members may be a means to participate in a youth culture and as mechanism for "getting by" (Klein, 1995, p. 26).

The heart of the issue is the conceptual link between gang life and criminal behavior. Klein states, "most gang members' behavior is not criminal, and most gang members' crimes are not violent" (1995, p. 29). Given the premise that criminal activity may constitute a small percentage of a gang's activities, is it appropriate to define a gang in terms of its illegal actions? When crime and youth gangs are linked, is delinquency more the product than the goal of gang members? Irrespective of this conceptual dispute, many people perceive gang members as an anti-social element.

Klein finds it useful to think of gangs-in-the-making as reaching "tipping points"—junctures in time where citizens begin to think of teenage groups as developing into gangs. Creating this transition are two factors. First, the group engages in a criminal orientation. To Klein, criminal orientation does not constitute "a pattern of serious criminal activity, as many in the enforcement world might require" (Klein, 1995, p. 30). Second, recognition of the group takes place, including special vocabularies, clothing, signs, and colors. At this point, social workers, school teachers, and community officials begin to discuss the existence of a troublesome gang. Next, the group acquires gang status in the community, is labeled as such, and eventually begins to interact with others similarly described.

Every youth group that engages in anti-social activities does not become a gang. Some are reluctant to adopt an overall criminal identity. In other cases, communities may be less inclined to label the group's action as "gang character" and may choose to address deviant behavior on an individual basis. Actually, in some instances, a lack of community recognition and response to an emerging gang's identity can downplay their prominence and undercut the growth of group cohesiveness.

What characterizes adolescents who join gangs? Who are these teenagers and how do they differ from other adolescents? Are gang members solely social outcasts and delinquents?

The answer to these questions may be disturbing. "Gang members are not so much different from other young people as they are caricatures of young people. Their needs and their pleasures are exaggerations of those familiar to us from a more general youth population" (Klein, 1995, p. 76). They comprise a wider variety of adolescents than often portrayed in mass media.

Gangs do not always include hoods, punks, and defiant personalities but may be comprised of teenagers who are insecure, aggressive, lonely, or sad. Gangs have leaders, followers, members on the periphery, and members needing to belong somewhere. Thus, a profile of gang members must encompass a broader spectrum of individuals than the stereotypic "tough guy" image.

With regard to the association between drugs and gangs, Klein states, "half the connection is pure hype; the other half exists and is worthy of attention along with other equally important gang issues, such as proliferation, crime patterns, ethnic variation, and approaches to control" (1995, p. 40). Media attention to crack-selling gangs has influenced the public to view gangs almost exclusively in terms of a drug-violence subculture. For many Americans, gangs and drug gangs are one and the same. Klein, however, asserts, "It just ain't so!... Gangs are lousy mechanisms for drug distribution...street gangs aren't well enough structured to suit the sellers' purpose" (1995, pp. 41–42). He concludes:

1. Use (of drugs) is far more common than sales;
2. Sales involvement on the whole is rather low;
3. There is enormous diversity between and within cities in the level of gang involvement in drug sales.
   (1995, p. 43)

The development of youth gangs is symptomatic of large-scale underlying social and economic problems in urban areas (Huff, 1989). So, the coexistence of gangs and a viable drug marketplace should not be a surprise.

Gang joiners tend to include one or more of the following descriptions:

- A notable set of personal deficiencies—perhaps difficulty in school, low self-esteem, lower impulse control, inadequate social skills, a deficit in useful adult contacts.
- A notable tendency toward defiance, aggressiveness, fighting, and pride in physical prowess.
- A greater-than-normal desire for status, identity, and companionship that can be at least partly satisfied by joining a special group like a gang.

- A boring, uninvolved lifestyle, in which the occasional excitement of gang exploits or rumored exploits provides a welcome respite. (Klein, 1995, p. 76)

Of all the reasons cited for participating in gang life, one of the most compelling is the need for belonging, for companionship, self-worth, or excitement (Clark, 1992). Were they not alienated at home, school, or from other peers, it is likely that these youth would be less inclined to drift toward gang involvement. For gang members, the gang life becomes family, a potent form of security.

Gangs do perform positive functions for some adolescents. Klein identifies four parts to the "gang-as-positive-mechanism philosophy." This philosophy suggests that gangs might: "facilitate their members' self-actualization," "provide local empowerment," "be coopted for social goals," and "serve to stabilize disorganized communities" (1995, pp. 82–85). To expect gangs to become positive forces in a community, however, is probably both naive and unrealistic, as the potential gains from gang membership are "too often counterbalanced by the damages of gang membership" (Klein, 1995, p. 85).

CASE EXAMPLE

Samuel Harris is a 55-year old African-American employed as a social worker at the Santa Louisa Community Center, located in a large city in the northeastern United States. This community center coordinates numerous programs for residents in this impoverished section of town—including a soup kitchen, a free store, a meals-on-wheels program, a health clinic, a day care facility, a Head Start program, and the teen outreach program. The Santa Louisa Community Center is conveniently located between a large housing project and the public middle and high schools.

For the past 15 years, Samuel, or "S" as he is known on the street, has worked as a community organizer in the neighborhood. His primary responsibilities include working with teenagers to encourage them to stay in school, seek job training, find employment, and stay out of trouble.

A brief overview of the neighborhood indicates a predominance of African-American, Hispanic American, and Italian American residents. Over half of the homes are female-headed, with most families receiving AFDC, food stamps, or public housing. Street life is a dominant feature in the neighborhood, with the existence of several gangs, organized around race and ethnicity. While crime has long been a problem in the community, recent years have seen a marked increase in all forms of crime.

Six months ago the neighborhood experienced a tragedy when Harold "Pop" Jones, an 80-year-old owner of a convenience store (and Samuel's close friend), was robbed and shot by a member of a newly formed gang. Pop was loved and respected by neighborhood residents, young and old, irrespective of race or ethnicity. Pop's Stop was more than a convenient market; it was a local landmark. While Pop was known for his cantankerous ways, his store was a popular place to buy snacks, catch up on local gossip, and see a familiar face. Pop sat on his stool at the front by the cash register, so as not to miss any activity in his store or on the street.

Since Pop's death, Samuel has observed two phenomena. First, disapproval of gang membership has increased among parents and adolescents. Pop's death caused people to observe youth and question them about ganglike activities. Even existing gangs have tried to distance themselves from the murder of this elderly man as well as from other forms of violent crime.

Second, Samuel's colleagues at the local juvenile justice center have observed an increase of non-gang-related petty crimes among teenagers. Teenagers began to hang out in or near several local pool halls, resulting in numerous arrests for disorderly conduct and petty theft. An initial assessment suggests that the timing might be ideal for engaging community teenagers in alternative activities. Court officials at Juvenile Hall expressed an interest in working with Samuel and others to divert teenagers from both the criminal justice system and gang life.

The shocking death of Harold "Pop" Jones attracted the attention of neighborhood residents, court officials, the city council, business leaders, and local media to the problems of teenagers in the area. At his funeral, family members asked that a foundation be established in Pop's name to benefit local youth. While Pop's Stop will not reopen, Samuel and others are moving quickly to assess the use of Pop Jones Foundation funds for developing community projects for adolescents.

TIME TO THINK!

Samuel has spent most of the past 15 years trying to improve the quality of life for residents served by the Santa Louisa Community Center. Samuel has a unique opportunity to address the needs of neighborhood adolescents more effectively. Brainstorming with community leaders provided Samuel with insight concerning macro-level issues to consider. For example, are macro-level interventions prejudged or discarded because the client population involves inner-city teenagers who have been in trouble with the law? Would the intervention modalities be different if the gangs were from middle-class, white neighborhoods? If so, in what ways? Finally, must a tragedy occur in order to prompt community reaction and analysis focusing on macro-level issues? What part could media take in sensitizing the community to the urgency of this situation? How could Samuel help to bring about such consciousness-raising?

MACRO SYSTEMS AND TROUBLED TEENAGERS

As we have said, a major emphasis in this book involves seeing the big picture in social work practice. While community organizers may be better trained to assess the influence of various macro-level systems, like all social workers they are not immune to influences of their own practice environment.

Samuel sees a special opportunity to develop programming to entice teenagers away from gang membership and street life. As we scan macro-level systems, a goal is to identify organizational, community, societal, and global factors that Samuel might fail to consider due to his closeness to the neighborhood and the emotional nature of the circumstances.

Organizational Level

In his practice at Santa Louisa, Samuel has developed relationships with various community organizations, including the local schools, Juvenile Hall, the police department, juvenile gangs, city government, and local businesses. He is a member of several interagency cluster groups examining adolescent problems and has served on numerous community task forces, including a now defunct anti-gang coalition formed five years ago.

Samuel's general observation is that organizations with the goal of confronting adolescents and teenage gangs often result only in uniting community teenagers against them. Meanwhile, entrepreneurs establish pool halls and teen nightclubs to profit from adolescents struggling with self-identity crises and an abundance of free time. As adolescents gravitate toward an activity (e.g., shooting pool, doing drugs, or hanging out at the club), they learn to identify with socially nonconforming groups (e.g., hoods, druggies, or clubbers). When their particular group becomes labeled as undesirable or deviant, negative self-esteem is further enhanced.

Two of the more productive community undertakings of Santa Louisa for adolescents are a teenage boxing club and a traveling basketball team called the "Rims." In both cases, former professional athletes from the area have volunteered time and money to provide healthy alternatives to teenagers in the community. While sponsored by several agencies, both of these programs were administered through the Santa Louisa Community Center.

By reading recent research, Samuel has become interested in innovative programs that reach out to teenagers in new ways. Fashimpar (1991) documents the merits of creative ventures like mini-bike clubs over the traditional approach of probation-casework or the deterrent effect of arrest. While a mini-bike club is probably unrealistic in Samuel's neighborhood, he senses encouragement, support, and a willingness from many organizations to examine fresh ways to reach out to teenagers. Innovative projects seeking Pop Jones Foundation monies, however, would need to both embrace the spirit of the foundation and form a consensus among participating organizations as to popular and appropriate activities for gaining teenage participation.

Community Level

The Santa Louisa Community Center is located in an area that can best be described as economically depressed. New jobs for adults and teenagers are virtually nonexistent in this section of town. For many residents, the local metro bus system is the only viable link to employment outside the community. Unfortunately, a centralized routing system makes bus transportation around the city both inefficient and time-consuming.

The dire socioeconomic climate of the community creates a feeling of pessimism for many adolescents. While Samuel has focused on finding jobs for teenagers in other parts of the city, employment opportunities are scarce. Potential employers often cite limited transportation as the reason for their reluctance to hire. Samuel believes another reason may be even more important: teenagers from his neighborhood have been labeled negatively by fast-food and service enterprises. Comments from prospective employers have been discouraging: "Your kids are too streetwise!" or "Why would I hire those teenagers when I can hire college-prep students?"

Samuel is deeply concerned about the negative image of the community. Recent media coverage has focused on gang life, crime, and welfare fraud. While several neighborhood churches offer adolescent support programs, they have received little recognition. Moreover, although group discussions, rap sessions, seminars, and gospel music groups organized by the churches appeal to only a segment of the adolescent population, these programs highlight positive attributes of community life and provide opportunities for adolescents to create constructive peer associations while avoiding negative labels.

Samuel is mindful that the community image can influence adolescent self-concept and self-esteem. In assessing program development, one priority is to promote a positive community outlook. Toward achieving this goal, Samuel favors using Pop Jones Foundation funds to promote activities that appeal to adolescents and still promote the community's image citywide.

Societal Level

Samuel is engaged in social work practice with adolescents who are trying to survive even as they seek growth and self-actualization despite bleak, dismal living conditions. When Samuel explains that he is a social worker involved in community organizing with teenagers in this neighborhood, people frequently ask what it is like working with "thugs and inner-city hoods." Samuel realizes that many are unable to look beyond social labels to see the pain and needs of others.

In the United States, impoverished "ghetto" sections of cities are seen as forms of cancer. Using this analogy, inhabitants of less desirable neighborhoods—the minority urban underclass—are seen as malignant cells to be removed by radical surgery. The strategy becomes to identify, isolate, and eliminate. Federal, state, and local officials express negative attitudes in both their attention and appropriations.

In the United States, highway systems are often constructed to avoid contact with this "cancer" or its cells. Suburban drivers speed by the "infected" areas of the city, refraining from even casual interaction with the "disease," hoping that it will not afflict them. If a cell is perceived as irregular or deviant, we move to label and isolate or eliminate, in the fear that "healthy cells" might be affected.

"The larger society certainly does label some minority persons, a priori, as 'probably deviant'...to be young, male, and black or Chicano in white America is to be a suspect person" (Moore, 1985, p. 2). Moore uses **ascribed deviance** to describe the labeling of a particular segment of the population based only on generalized minority stereotypes.

Samuel knows that ascribed deviance exists. Call it racism, discrimination, or prejudice, teenagers from impoverished areas are viewed differently and as inferior. Samuel must deal with these societal attitudes each day, as he sees teenagers doubt their worth and turn toward negative alternatives.

International Level

As part of a large metropolitan city in the northeastern United States, the Santa Louisa Community Center has experienced a steady flow of first-generation Hispanic American immigrants into the community. As a result, Samuel attempts to familiarize himself with the ways of each ethnic group in order to keep abreast of various cultural influences on teenagers.

Samuel has found interesting distinctions with regard to clothing, music, and value orientations that distinguish African-American, Hispanic American, and Italian American adolescents. In some sections of the community one needs only to look at the graffiti and listen to the beat of the music to ascertain the ethnic origin of the residents.

Samuel has recently discovered that the murder of his friend Pop Jones was by the hand of a member wearing the colors of a newly formed gang, housed in a bordering community. Hoping to "take new turf," this white youth gang has been associated with several violent acts in the city.

Samuel is familiar with the violent reputation of youth gangs and has learned that many of them link their identity to street gangs and criminal syndicates from years past (Klein, 1995, p. 217). He has made a special effort to learn about the historical and cultural foundations of the ethnic and racial gangs in the neighborhood. Samuel has an added advantage in being fluent in several languages used in the community.

APPLYING A SOCIAL WORK FRAMEWORK: LABELING THEORY

In this chapter, labeling theory is introduced as an appropriate theoretical orientation for assessing developmental issues during adolescence. Our intent is to encourage readers to focus on social reactions to teenagers rather than to concentrate on adolescent behaviors and actions. Social workers must consider the consequences of labeling teenagers as undesirable, deviants, punks, druggies, and gang members. This chapter demonstrates a layering effect with regard to social labels. Teenagers can be stigmatized, at one or more levels, as individuals, group members, members of subcultures or minority groups, residents of a community, or any combination of these. The significance of labeling at each tier lies in its potential for generating distinctive lifestyles (secondary deviance) for teenagers, as labeling evokes images of deviance (Moore, 1985, p. 1).

In this chapter's case example, Samuel assesses mechanisms for breaking down existing social labels and for creating positive teenage alternatives. Teenagers need to connect with affirming, healthful activities and groups. Samuel has seen too many adolescents from his neighborhood enter the criminal justice system. Those in power quickly judge, incarcerate, and forget the life that needs rebuilding. Pop Jones's death created an opportunity to rally residents and community leaders into action to change this cycle.

As labeling theory dictates, Samuel Harris strives to identify and accentuate the strengths of neighborhood adolescents at every turn. Choosing to deemphasize legal confrontation, Samuel and other social workers in the neighborhood hope to use Pop Jones Foundation funds to offer original and responsive programs.

─────────────── **SUGGESTED ACTIVITIES** ───────────────

1. Visit the city or county juvenile court. What are your impressions of the building, people, and atmosphere? Is it possible to differentiate between first-time and repeat offenders? How do these individuals differ? Are there people who seem very familiar with the court while others appear to be newcomers?

2. Interview a social worker at a community center serving adolescents. Inquire about the clientele, community needs, and programs currently offered. Ask the social worker to identify the primary public misconception about teenagers in the area.

3. Talk to an adolescent relative about different student groupings at her or his school; mention grunge. Let the adolescent describe and articulate the characteristics of as many groups as possible. Ask also about the presence of any gangs at school. Let the adolescent be the expert and you be the listener.

138

REFERENCES

Alden, G. (1993). The Remains of Grunge. *Rolling Stone*, January 21, 48-49.

Al-Talib, N., & Griffin, C. (1994). Labeling Effect on Adolescents' Self-Concept. *International Journal of Offender Therapy and Comparative Criminology*, 38(1), 47-57.

Aronson, E. (1972). *The Social Animal*. San Francisco: W.H. Freeman and Company.

Becker, H. (1963). *Outsiders: Studies in the Sociology of Deviance*. New York: The Free Press.

Becker, H. (1964). *The Other Side: Perspectives on Deviance*. New York: The Free Press.

Binder, A., & Geis, G. (1984). Ad Populum Argumentation in Criminology: Juvenile Diversion as Rhetoric. *Crime and Delinquency*, 30(4), 624-647.

Borzillo, C. (1994). Cobain Mourned by Fans, Industryites in Memorials, Music Stores. *Billboard*, April 23, 102.

Carnegie Council on Adolescent Development (1996). *Great Transitions: Preparing Adolescents for a New Century*. New York: Carnegie Corporation of New York.

Clark, C. (1992). Deviant Adolescent Subcultures: Assessment Strategies and Clinical Interventions. *Adolescence*, 27(106), 283-293.

Fashimpar, G. (1991). From Probation to Mini-bikes: A Comparison of Traditional and Innovative Programs for Community Treatment of Delinquent Adolescents. *Social Work with Groups*, 14(2), 105-118.

Horwitz, A., & Wasserman, M. (1979). The Effect of Social Control on Delinquent Behavior: A Longitudinal Test. *Sociological Focus*, 12(1), 53-70.

Huff, R. (1989). Youth Gangs and Public Policy. *Crime and Delinquency*, 35(4), 524-537.

Kaplan, H., & Fukurai, J. (1992). Negative Social Sanctions, Self-Rejection, and Drug Use. *Youth and Society*, 23(3), 275-298.

Kaplan, H., & Johnson, R. (1991). Negative Social Sanctions and Juvenile Delinquency: Effects of Labeling in a Model of Deviant Behavior. *Social Science Quarterly*, 72(1), 98-122.

Kate, N. (1995). Squeaky Clean Teens. *American Demographics*, 17(1), 42–43.

Klein, M. (1995). *The American Street Gang*. New York: Oxford University Press.

Lemert, E. (1951). *Social Pathology*. New York: McGraw-Hill Book Company.

Lieberman, R. (1993). Springtime for Grunge. *Artforum*, 31(8), 8–10.

Matsueda, R. (1992). Reflected Appraisals, Parental Labeling, and Delinquency: Specifying a Symbolic Interactionist Theory. *American Journal of Sociology*, 97(6), 1577–1611.

Moore, J. (1985). Isolation and Stigmatization in the Development of an Underclass: The Case of Chicano Gangs in East Los Angeles. *Social Problems*, 33(1), 1–12.

Morash, M. (1982). Juvenile Reaction to Labels: An Experiment and an Exploratory Study. *Sociology and Social Research*, 67(1), 76–88.

Morash, M. (1983). Groups, Gangs, and Delinquency. *British Journal of Criminology*, 4, 316.

New York Times (1995). Rock Star's Forum Grows Too Raucous for On-line Service, April 12, 19.

Palamara, F., Cullen, F., & Gersten, J. (1986). The Effect of Police and Mental Health Intervention on Juvenile Deviance: Specifying Contingencies in the Impact of Formal Reaction. *Journal of Health and Social Behavior*, 27, 90–105.

Pipher, M. (1994). *Reviving Ophelia: Saving the Selves of Adolescent Girls*. New York: Ballantine Books.

Rosenbaum, J., & Prinsky, L. (1991). The Presumption of Influence: Recent Responses to Popular Music Subcultures. *Crime and Delinquency*, 37(4), 528–535.

Sherman, L., & Berk, R. (1984). The Specific Deterrent Effects of Arrest for Domestic Assault. *American Sociological Review*, 49, 261–272.

Shilts, L. (1991). The Relationship of Early Adolescent Substance Use to Extracurricular Activities, Peer Influence, and Personal Attitudes. *Adolescence*, 26(103), 613–616.

Stager, S., Chassin, L., & Young, R. (1983). Determinants of Self-Esteem Among Labeled Adolescents. *Social Psychology Quarterly*, 46(1), 3–10.

Steitz, J., & Owen, T. (1992). School Activities and Work: Effects on Adolescent Self-Esteem. *Adolescence*, 27(105), 37–50.

Thomas, C., & Bishop, D. (1984). The Effect of Formal and Informal Sanctions on Delinquency: A Longitudinal Comparison of Labeling and Deterrence Theories. *The Journal of Criminal Law and Criminology*, 75(4), 1222–1245.

Thrasher, F. (1967). *The Gang: A Study of 1,313 Gangs in Chicago*. Chicago: University of Chicago Press.

Traub, S., & Little, C. (1975). Labeling and Deviance. In S. Traub and C. Little (Eds.), *Theories of Deviance*. Itasca, IL: F.E. Peacock Publishers.

6

Young Adulthood

"Cathy," a syndicated cartoon character found in the comic section of many newspapers, is a young single adult in a fictional world. She reflects a segment of working women who struggle with identity and coping issues. This daily comic strip is dedicated to the humorous trials and tribulations of Cathy's work, her dating, her ever-ticking biological clock, and her ambivalent relationship with her parents.

Cathy, like many young adults, is continually anxious about her body image. She spends hours deliberating about life's difficult choices: how to achieve the "right" appearance, create the most attractive body image, and choose clothes to enhance that image. She struggles with the problem of relationships with coworkers, men, and her parents. An emerging adult, Cathy is rarely satisfied with herself and seeks reassurance from others at nearly every turn. In her quest for independence, she vacillates between seeking her parents' approval and wanting to define her own person. Indeed, Cathy is in a perpetual, modern-day frenzy.

Cathy appeals to a wide audience in the United States as young women identify with her relentless introspection and difficulty with everyday decision making. Yet, does Cathy portray

141

CATHY © Cathy Guisewite. Reprinted with permission of UNIVERSAL PRESS SYNDICATE. All rights reserved.

reality? Does she reflect a perception of common issues facing young adults in our society? Does Cathy typify the conflicts of young adults in the '90s?

In the exaggerated manner of television and movies, the comic strip often portrays life as a carefree journey without economic or social limitations. Like many middle- and upper-class individuals, Cathy is able to make choices concerning work, clothes, personal relationships, and residence. Many of Cathy's readers may view these choices as a normal way of life for most young adult Americans. But this is a comic strip, not reality. Many less fortunate Americans do not have money for a daily newspaper and would deny that Cathy's turmoil in any way reflects the dilemmas of the poor.

Cathy is a white, privileged young adult, oblivious to the plight of African-Americans, Hispanic Americans, and other persons of color in America. She does not frequent neighborhoods characterized by high crime and drug trafficking. The economic and social decline experienced by northern industrial cities has little impact on Cathy's perception of life or social well being.

Cathy has not yet confronted important issues of the '90s such as sexual orientation, job discrimination, or the AIDS epidemic. Yet, to equate a comic strip with reality is certainly to make an improper comparison. After all, Cathy is a fictional creation intended to entertain and amuse the reader, and to provide escape from reality. However, these daily strips provide commentary on significant social issues.

THEORY: VALUE CONFLICT

In this chapter we have chosen a value-conflict orientation for viewing young adulthood. While other theories could be of equal importance or merit with regard to this developmental period, we feel that this perspective will enliven discussion.

Value-conflict theory focuses explicitly on environmental conditions rather than on individual behaviors (Hardert, Gordon, Laner, and Reader, 1984, p. 14). This theory asserts that certain groups of people in our society espouse specific value-centered positions. Groups that organize around a special interest often find themselves directly in competition with other groups attempting to define social realities and policies. DiNitto (1995) contends that it is the exception when social values are agreed upon in a societal context. Instead, it is typical that groups will have conflicting values. She suggests:

1. Defining social problems is difficult. People do not agree on what constitutes a social problem, since what may be a social problem for one group may be a benefit for another.
2. Groups differ in their power and ability to advance a special interest.
3. Policy makers are motivated less by social values and more by the potential to maximize rewards given by special interest organizations. (DiNitto, 1995, pp. 8–9)

Affirmative action initiatives provide examples of value conflicts. Civil rights activists argue that without concrete plans for mandating the employment of underrepresented groups of people in the U.S. labor force, advancement for minorities in the workplace will be either nonexistent or staggeringly slow. Business groups, however, hold that affirmative action policies restrict individual choices and undermine a free economic system, creating a burden for employers.

From a value-conflict orientation, various special interest or value-centered groups compete, politically and socially, for their own points of view and rights. Each group hopes to define reality from its vested-interest position. The goal for each group, if it is powerful enough, is to define the other group and its stance as deviant.

As a result of the proliferation of special interest groups, laws regulating lobbying groups have been enacted in the United States. Such legislation requires special interests to identify themselves when acting as political lobbying entities, and it defines what constitutes acceptable lobbying activity. While there is considerable debate concerning the net impact of this kind of regulation, the need to monitor and provide oversight with regard to the behavior of special interest groups is evident (Lowery and Gray, 1994).

DEVELOPMENTAL ISSUES

Lidz's (1976) classic work, *The Person*, depicts young adulthood as a life-cycle phase, usually between the ages of 18 and 35, filled with important choices. These choices include marriage, occupation, and parenting. While Lidz (1976, p. 81) clearly recognized the influence of family and peers with respect to life expectations and tasks, are parenting, marriage, and occupation to be considered merely individual choices?

People make daily choices that affect their lives. Individuals, to varying degrees, are able to consider life circumstances, to actively set goals, and to plot the pathways that they wish to pursue. However, to more fully enter the world of the client, the social worker needs an in-depth appreciation of social influences, restraints, and parameters that facilitate or curtail personal choices.

Social class distinctions affect employment, marital status, and parenting. Is the Cinderella story reality? Is it typical for poor Americans to be courted by the economic elite in business or marriage? Scan your classroom. Are you sitting next to a Rockefeller or a Kennedy? Do you attend parties and other functions with those from privileged segments of our society? Have you entered a career in which you will rub elbows with the movers and shakers of our society? Rather, might you identify with the poor and homeless, the hungry, the mentally and physically disabled, and the impoverished of our world?

Clearly, we live in a segregated society where social inequality and injustice are implicit—if not explicit—elements in the daily lives of people in the United States (South and Deane, 1993). It would be naive to assert that young adults choose a community in which to live, select a career, commit to a spouse, or decide upon the number of children they will bear solely on the basis of cognitive functioning and desire (Rosenbaum, 1994).

As a social worker, you will meet clients who have several children, but who do not understand how children are conceived. Other clients may be knowledgeable about human reproduction but lack specific information concerning birth control. To assume that all young adults in the United States make cognitive, informed choices about parenting is erroneous. Instead, many children in our society are conceived out of ignorance, misinformation, or emotion.

A major challenge for novice social workers is setting aside one's personal experiences and avoiding case generalizations about clients of a similar age. Each young adult has been uniquely influenced by sets of person-specific social influences and systems and by individual circumstances. Unfortunately, recent research suggests that some social workers overemphasize personal choice as an explanation for human behavior (McDonell, 1993). Therefore, the social worker must assess the impact of particular groups, organizations, the neighborhood, the community, and societal norms while remaining alert to a tendency to "blame the victim" and to demand a higher degree of personal responsibility than the client is capable of assuming.

As an example, not every student has been prepared to enter college. And not all young adults can afford the high costs of higher education. The school that one attends during primary and secondary education has an enormous impact on the individual's educational aspirations, future academic opportunities, and view of life (Palmer and Little, 1993, p. 316). Children do not choose to be born into a particular family, neighborhood, or social status. As a result of socioeconomic circumstances, parents are often unable to choose the school they want their children to attend or to consider higher education for their offspring (Stolzenberg, 1994). Many factors are beyond individual control during young adulthood.

INTERRELATIONSHIPS OF DEVELOPMENTAL ISSUES

The remainder of this chapter focuses on dilemmas young adults routinely face with regard to marriage, parenting, and occupation or career attainment. While each developmental issue is examined separately, these topics are related. As before, our emphasis is on the macro-level social systems and their pervasive influence on life stages.

The manner in which our society focuses on the virtue of marriage as a prerequisite to parenting provides a helpful illustration. Expectations concerning the timing, occurrence, and sequence of marriage and childbearing are an important component of American culture (Trent, 1994). As an example, premarital childbearing is often viewed as an inappropriate transition during young adulthood and one that contributes to the persistence of poverty in America. The more traditional and acceptable sequence of events is to marry and then to coordinate childrearing with occupational aspirations.

Marriage, parenting, and occupation are interconnected. As you read this chapter, you can construct examples that emphasize the interdependent nature on these life events.

Marriage

Typically, books examining young adulthood and marriage focus on issues of self-identity, parental influences, attraction, dating, and marital happiness (Zastrow and Kirst-Ashman, 1990). While these are certainly important topics, let's examine some additional macro-level considerations for social workers with respect to marriage during young adulthood.

SEXUAL ORIENTATION The mushrooming issue of homosexuality has altered the typical textbook approach to marriage. New issues become paramount. Can two young adults choose to get married? If they are of legal age, the obvious answer is yes—if they are of the opposite sex. The debate regarding homosexual marriages has been prolonged, but most states either prohibit or do not recognize marriage between consenting adults of the same sex. Businesses reflect a similar perspective, a fact most observable in company policies regarding health and retirement benefits. Religious groups continue the ethical debate regarding gay and lesbian couples.

Even for some social workers, the idea of a homosexual couple or family presents an enigma, a conceptual leap. As a result, the social worker must consider the psychosocial impact of discrimination against homosexuals and bisexuals during young adulthood. Love, irrespective of sexual orientation, involves excitement, emotion, and passion. People in love want to express their feelings for each other, not sublimate their emotions to conform to society's norms.

The institution of traditional marriage in the United States has been defended by heterosexual, religious, or politically conservative persons and special interest groups, who find it difficult to accept the ideas of domestic same-sex partnerships and especially of gay marriage. For homosexuals and lesbians who wish to publicly proclaim their love and committed relationships, society has until recently continued to hold the closet door tightly closed. The "coming out" movement initiated by gay and lesbian organizations demonstrates an organized effort that lobbies for the rights of people to openly and freely express their love for a person of the same sex.

The desire for long-term relationships is common to a majority of homosexual couples (Longres, 1995). The expression of love within a legal, socially approved setting is the hope of many gay and lesbian couples, who continue to push social boundaries as they demand legitimizing of their lifestyle.

In addition to traditional lifelong marriage there are five other arrangements:

1. Staying single—never marrying
2. Living together—cohabitation
3. Marrying, then divorcing
4. Divorcing, marrying someone else
5. Homosexual partnerships

Persons in our society involved in nontraditional relationships often compete for equal opportunities and legitimacy. Employers, for example, may offer jobs or promotions to individuals because they view them as "family types" having family members to support. Imagine the added difficulties in becoming a leader in community youth groups, running for local political office, or securing a loan for a home if one is engaged in a homosexual relationship.

Single or divorced people, as well as homosexuals, often sense a public perception of themselves as losers or social rejects. Seeking understanding, these people congregate in the basements of churches and temples, in public meeting areas, or wherever space is available to unite, explore mutual needs, and advocate for their common rights and benefits.

DIVERSITY IN MARRIAGE Those who fall in love with people different from themselves in race, nationality, age, and religion face unique social pressures and constraints in life. While many will argue that people who enter heterogeneous types of marriages should realize the potential for social discord, love knows few bounds. People are emotional, fall in love, and often hope their love will be immune to the prejudices and beliefs of others.

In social work practice, your clients will reflect a wide range of social associations and arrangements in their intimate relationships. The challenge is to be sensitive in understanding and appreciating each type of relationship and to become familiar with community and national organizations available to address special needs.

WIVES AND DEPENDENCY We would be remiss, however, in exploring alternatives to the institution of marriage in the United States if we failed to acknowledge the continued plight of many women in heterosexual marriages (Vannoy-Hiller and Philliber, 1989). While adult gender roles are changing and women may have "come a long way, baby," women and men often enter marriage without equality. Many women in heterosexual relationships find themselves economically and socially less powerful and overly dependent on men. An aggressive woman in our society may be labeled "a bitch," while an aggressive man is seen as a "go-getter" or overachiever. Often, automobile salespersons talk to the husband about the car and offer refreshments to the wife and children. In many marriages women have not reached full partnership with men.

Through organizations such as the National Organization for Women (NOW), women have come together to confront the many "super women" expectations placed upon females in our society, as well as to demand equal pay and recognition in the workforce. Women's organizations have been historically important in raising issues, demanding change, and in counseling women. During the mid-1880s in urban areas of the United States women organized for the right to vote. Later women banded together to achieve full legal, social, economic, and educational equality. Their efforts continue in their struggle for liberation from sexual harassment and gender stereotyping. The establishment of professional networks (legal, medical, economic) has enabled women to define their special needs in gender-specific ways.

When women see their family physicians or therapists because they feel depressed, controlled, and/or discontented in their marriages, they frequently encounter a variety of responses. Traditionally, male doctors have interpreted these complaints as depression. The treatment suggested is often antidepressant drugs such as Prozac (Cowley, 1994). Yet the physical complaints may be signs of a need to gain social power in relationships and/or to seek avenues of recourse for involvement in the broader cause of improving conditions not only for themselves but for all women.

For women, as for any other special interest group, power is necessary to apply the political and social muscle required for social change. Improved domestic conditions for women occur as a result of social movements by people who are organized to support and bring about change. Although antidepressant therapies have clinical importance for treatment with certain diagnoses, they are not prescriptions for social change.

A traditionally cited prerequisite for such changes is the involvement of a few powerful people, or many less powerful individuals, confronting a specific social problem or cause (McKee and Robertson, 1975). Therefore, it is important for women to support women's causes actively, to gain strength collectively, and to identify new directions for creating change.

Women, regardless of social class, experience loss of self-esteem, may feel controlled, and in some cases experience physical abuse in marriage. Publicity surrounding the death of Nicole Brown Simpson and the alleged domestic violence in her relationship with O.J. Simpson brought this issue to national attention. The suffering and pain of one well-known woman served to awaken a nation to an important social issue affecting many women.

A pivotal dilemma for the social worker to explore with each client involves personal problem versus social problem. Does your client seek mental health, membership in a social cause, physical protection, or all of the above? Have you as a social worker assessed both the macro and micro elements of a particular case and considered social change as well as personal change?

Parenting

Parenting issues for young adults include the reasons people have children, when to have children, how to parent, and choosing not to have children (Papalia and Olds, 1989). Each of these topics focuses on intrapsychic aspects of the phenomenon. Here, we consider the social conditions that surround and influence having children.

PARENTHOOD AND PLANNING Should parenthood be planned or unplanned? Contraception, artificial insemination, adoption, and surrogate parenting all involve rational approaches. In these instances, people wish to be parents and utilize time-consuming and expensive processes to achieve that goal. Similarly, if a young adult practices abstinence, the decision not to have children is implicit.

While modern technology has provided us with an array of birth control measures for planning parenthood, birth control is problematic and involves important qualifiers. Birth control pills, diaphragms, and condoms, for example, are readily available. However, effective use of birth control devices assumes not only availability but knowledge and education concerning standard procedures for using each method. The person who is able to follow instructions for using a birth control device greatly enhances his or her opportunity for successfully planning parenthood.

Accurate and straight talk concerning birth control, sterilization, and sexually transmitted diseases varies from family to family, school to school, and community to community. Now with the impact of AIDS, individuals may be more willing to speak openly and freely about sex and birth control. However, books and manuals on sex education still have restricted access in those libraries that fear violating community or societal norms. As Federico (1990) suggests, sex education must go well beyond the biological aspects of sex. As social workers you will often need to explore with clients the relationship between human sexuality and individual aspirations, economic stability, and lifestyle issues, knowing that this dialogue might not occur elsewhere.

Sex education and planned parenting are emotionally laden subjects for many Americans. At one end of the continuum, certain religious and political groups lobby in favor of sex education being taught exclusively in the family rather than in the classroom. These groups may also view abortion as murder and advocate that it be outlawed. They organize protests and picket at family planning and abortion clinics to champion their position.

Conversely, planned-parent organizations and pro-choice organizations seek to openly disseminate information concerning procreation, birth control, and abortion to women of childbearing age. Groups like NOW sponsor marches, rallies, and forums to promote women's rights to make their own reproductive choices.

Moreover, parenting is a social-class issue. If individuals possess the necessary knowledge and resources to effectively implement birth control, then parenting is likely to involve a rational, planned choice. But if sexually active individuals lack the information or do not have the resources to secure birth control devices, then parenting becomes a random event.

CHANGING SOCIAL POLICY TO INFLUENCE PARENTING Many states are examining the implementation of policies that would reduce or eliminate Aid to Families with Dependent Children (AFDC) benefits based on the current number of dependents. If, for example, a woman already has one child on AFDC, each subsequent child would either not qualify or qualify at a substantially lower rate for those benefits.

On the surface, such a policy would appear to act as a disincentive for AFDC mothers to have more children, assuming a rational model for birth control. However, who would be hurt by this type of policy, mother or child? This appears to be very punitive legislation. Single mothers in the United States already fare worse than single mothers in other countries (Wong, Garfinkel, and McLanahan, 1993). Is the movement to reduce AFDC rolls being spearheaded by special interest groups searching for ways to enable mothers to better provide for their children or by lobbies interested in finding ways for wealthier Americans to pay lower taxes? What other motives may be driving this discussion?

PROMOTING EFFECTIVE PARENTING Parenting is a complex task, requiring information, insight, skills, and emotional stability. Fortunately, a variety of organizations can help provide young adults with basic information, social support, and advocacy services to promote healthy parenting. Most child and family service agencies sponsor parenting seminars and classes in local communities. School-based programs, church-supported workshops, YWCA classes, single-parent clubs, child support enforcement agencies, Parents of Murdered Children (PMOC), Sudden Infant Death Syndrome (SIDS) chapters, Mothers Against Drunk Drivers (MADD), the Alliance for the Mentally Ill (AMI), and many others instruct, support, and counsel parents who face special needs or concerns related to parenting.

In assessing the social environment of a young adult, social workers should be aware of the function that special interest groups for parents can play in the life of the client. Parents of children with special needs often join social action organizations whose main purpose is to protect the child and link parents in similar situations with one another. These organizations, via meetings and newsletters, provide parents with recent research findings, social support, and an organized setting for exploring advocacy issues to benefit their children and families.

As an example, advocacy groups have recently become a significant force for change in laws affecting children and are active lobbyists for child mental health issues. Imagine the stresses facing a family or parent of a child who is mentally ill. Loneliness and bitterness are common emotions experienced by these persons. Organizations like AMI help parents to realize that they are not alone. People in need benefit from knowing that they may share common concerns.

AMI assists parents to be aware of legislation, existing or pending, that may affect their children. AMI members are regular participants and sponsors at mental health meetings and functions. They serve as strong voices on mental health issues, advancing the views of consumers with regard to future directions for mental health policies and programs.

In a similar fashion, family preservation movements across the country have initiated programs to provide timely and effective services for parents to keep at-risk children in home environments (Berry, 1992). Early assessment and intervention in these programs bring valuable problem-solving techniques and adaptation skills to parents.

Work

A fundamental value orientation for people in the United States involves the American work ethic. At an early age, children are socialized to believe that work is healthful, wholesome, and a major source of personal identity. At the next party or social gathering you attend, be an active listener and direct your attention to the conversation of people around you. Your friends and acquaintances will probably be discussing their academic major, job, or career aspirations. Irrespective of socioeconomic class, race, or gender, most young adults view work not just as a functional necessity but as defining who we are. While Americans learn to value work, we are also socialized to view certain types of occupations as more gender appropriate than others. If you doubt this premise, consider this anecdote from the recent past:

> A man and his son are traveling down a narrow road at night and become involved in a car accident. The son is seriously injured and taken to the closest hospital for immediate medical care. As the father and son enter the hospital, they are separated and the boy is taken to the emergency room. The attending emergency room doctor looks at the boy and quickly proclaims, "I can't treat this boy; he is my son!" How can this be?

Many people have guessed that the physician is the boy's stepfather and are surprised to find that the emergency room doctor is the boy's mother. Childhood stories, television, and other media reinforce gender stereotypes.

This exercise illustrates social boundaries and parameters that affect attainment of certain occupations by people in the

United States. Typically, literature describing human development during young adulthood focuses on occupational choice as a major developmental task. Yet, occupational choice assumes that people are actually free and able to pursue a particular career, profession, or vocation of their liking. Unfortunately, research indicates that gender, race, socioeconomic class, sexual orientation, disability, nationality, and other social statuses serve as social barriers that inhibit entry into a chosen field (Jacobsen, 1994) and contribute to salary inequities (Kilbourne, England, and Beron, 1994).

In our society it is often only the economically advantaged who can afford to attend the prestigious undergraduate universities and accumulate the years of graduate school education necessary to hold many professional positions. In the United States, licensing and certification requirements serve a gate-keeping function that allows certain members of our society to enter and turns others away.

Standards required for admission into many helping professions routinely lead to rejection of many applicants. As a result of marketplace demands and self-imposed professional control, application for a job opening is often restricted to individuals holding a special license or degree. The field of psychology presents a useful example. In most states, the practice of clinical psychology requires a Ph.D. or Psy.D. And while there are an appreciable number of doctoral degree programs in psychology in the United States, entry is restricted. It is difficult to gain admission into a doctoral program in clinical psychology because applicants far outnumber the limited number of openings available for students.

As an undergraduate or graduate student in social work, could you choose to enter a doctoral program in psychology? If you experience some misgivings or hesitancy at this question, imagine the sense of hopelessness that many of your clients feel with respect to meaningful employment and upward job mobility. If your client is mentally disabled or has special needs, you will need to understand the pain, frustration, and social barriers that come with seeking employment beyond beginning-level or service-oriented positions.

KNOWLEDGE OF SPECIAL INTERESTS As a social worker, you will be able to unite with colleagues to forward the special interests of both clients and social workers. The National Association of Social Workers (NASW) and its political action committee (PACE) represent two of these possibilities. In addition, the Council on Social Work Education (CSWE) and social work clinical associations constitute professional organizations that provide information about and advocate for the role of social work in the labor force.

Labor unions and professional associations in the United States have historically played vital roles in protecting the rights of workers and in formulating and shaping important social policies (Marmor, 1973). Young adults are probably unfamiliar with labor reforms (e.g., policies promoting healthy and safe working conditions or fair wage and medical benefits for workers) that were initiated and supported by organizations like the AFL-CIO, the Teamsters, and the United Auto Workers (Western, 1994).

Because young adults are still relatively new to the world of work and have not yet attained seniority in the labor force, they are especially vulnerable to manipulation and exploitation in their employment. Ironically, youth sometimes affords significant advantages as companies downsize. Preference is often given to younger workers who can be hired at lower salaries while laying off more expensive older workers. Other young adults fall victim to the "last hired/first fired" pattern. When young adults do not comply with the expectations of the employer, they face swift termination. Availability of applicants waiting to fill a position places the burden on the new worker to meet the demands of management or fear loss of her or his job.

Thus, for the social worker, knowledge concerning organizations and programs dedicated to promoting and protecting the rights of young adults in the labor force is paramount. Community-based employment education and training programs help young adults prepare for and seek meaningful work. Equal opportunity commissions, the National Urban

League, women-in-work conferences, labor unions, and professional associations constitute a few examples of potentially powerful allies available to clients.

Companies implement policies concerning day care provisions, flexible time, and fair rights hearings when forced to see the need and the benefits to the company. It takes organization for individuals and groups to demand these employment practices. Where is the young client with respect to participation in work-related groups and forums that focus attention on specific employment issues or needs? As a social worker, you will need to be informed about and involved in activities that emphasize empowering clients who enter the labor force.

CASE EXAMPLE

David Hewan is a 27-year-old, third-year engineering student at Florida State University (FSU). David's current grade point average is 3.5 out of a possible 4.0. During the past several months, however, David's grades have dropped. David appears sad. The student counseling center at FSU made a preliminary diagnosis of depression.

A social history reveals that David grew up in Jamaica in the small town of Sandy Bay, several miles west of the active tourist port of Montego Bay. David's father has been a tour bus driver for many years; his mother is a secretary in Immigration Services at the airport. David has one younger sister, Denise, aged 14. David is the only member of his immediate family who has left Jamaica.

As a child growing up on this Caribbean island, David was very fortunate to have attended private primary and secondary schools in Montego Bay. Following secondary school, David completed high school, fulfilling the first part of a lifelong dream of his parents.

Since he was six, David's parents saved money to enable him to attend college. Funds were deposited regularly in the bank for David's education. This involved many sacrifices and hardships for his parents, who lived a meager life in a simple and sparsely furnished home.

The plan had always been for David to come to the United States, where he could live with his maternal uncle, Cameron, and attend FSU. Because attaining a visa for study abroad is very difficult in Jamaica, it took David's parents over two years of political maneuvering to secure an educational visa for him. They agreed he would live with Cameron while in the United States and return to Jamaica following graduation.

While experiencing academic success at FSU, David's social experiences have been confusing and a source of personal turmoil. Though David appreciates living in the United States with his uncle and enjoys the many modern conveniences of his new home, he is aware of changes within himself. He is becoming more ambivalent about his eventual return to Jamaica. He often feels pleased about being a successful student who is quickly learning American customs. At the same time he experiences a sense of guilt at losing his Jamaican ways and roots. A promising career and an enduring relationship with his girlfriend, Juanita, are dependent upon living in the United States. Yet, David is continually troubled by his promise to return to Jamaica.

David yearns to stay in the United States, yet he feels the pull of his parents' expectations. Would he be disloyal not to return to his beloved Jamaica where his engineering knowledge and skills could be a significant asset to his country in its need for advanced technology? Would failure to return to his homeland be interpreted as the breaking of his word? Keeping one's promises and honoring fiscal responsibilities are values highly regarded by his parents.

In addition, David feels that if he stays in the United States, he stands to lose his identity as a Jamaican. He resents being referred to as a person of color or an African-American. He is a Jamaican! For this young man to be called anything else negates his sense of being and the heritage of his proud people.

At an early age, David learned the symbolism of the colors of the Jamaican flag. The green is for Jamaica's abundant vegetation, the yellow represents the sun that shines over Jamaica's land and sea, and the black symbolizes the hardships and struggles that the Jamaican people have endured. How can David forget his family, country, and people? Once life seemed to be "no problem"; now life seems just too difficult.

TIME TO THINK!

David presents a fairly common dilemma for people who come to the United States from other countries. While he appears distraught by intrapsychic conflict, what macro-level issues are germane to his case? How is your thinking influenced by the fact that David comes from Jamaica? Are there national or international considerations that might be appropriate to consider in your assessment? Though many of David's concerns are related to cross-cultural issues, which life-stage issues are similar to those of any other young adult?

MACRO SYSTEMS AND DAVID

Our goal is to encourage social workers to incorporate macro-level issues and factors into their daily routine when working with clients. With David as your client, you are challenged to explore organizational, community, societal, and global considerations.

Organizational Level

As a student at FSU, David is strongly influenced by the policies and programs of this institution of higher education. Thus, it would be beneficial to know about the presence of student organizations and/or university programs designed specifically to assist international students. Many universities have developed student organizations, clubs, and support programs designed to address the unique needs of such students. We know that David has family in Florida and the FSU area. We do not know about contacts with organizations David's family has made in the community. Does Cameron belong to any clubs or civic organizations that might interest David or provide assistance?

One should find out about Jamaican or Caribbean organizations in the community that provide opportunities for socializing, mutual support, and acquiring information. The local Traveler's Aid Society may be of assistance. Additionally, listings of agencies in the yellow pages or directories of community agencies often provide such information. Churches serving the neighborhood may also offer programs and insight concerning available resources.

What do we know about David's interests and priorities in life? Does he have a religious affiliation, participate in athletics (e.g., cricket and soccer are popular sports in Jamaica), or enjoy a musical interest? Does David attend a church, play on an athletic team, or belong to a musical group? These are areas to explore as the worker takes a social history. What are David's interests in the political process; is he interested in political advocacy or in joining a political action group?

As a social worker, view David's case as an opportunity to become familiar with Jamaican culture, mores, and organizations. In the United States there are travel agencies specializing in Jamaica. Travel centers, libraries, and government bureaus dealing with immigration could be important sources of information. A resourceful worker will gain increased insight from organizations that can contribute to a better understanding of the social/cultural framework.

Community Level

While David attends FSU, he lives with Uncle Cameron in the city of Conway, located just west of Tallahassee. It is important to examine the match between David and the community in which he lives. Florida, specifically the Tallahassee vicinity, is accustomed to sharing daily life with people from other countries and with diverse cultural backgrounds. David feels comfortable living with his Uncle Cameron. People of the city have made him feel welcome.

David's girlfriend, Juanita, is employed as a leasing representative in a nearby apartment community. Because Juanita is Spanish American, most local acquaintances initially believed that David also belonged to this ethnic group. When David first moved to live with Cameron, he was quick to correct people and to identify himself as Jamaican. Usually this did not present difficulties for David, as most people only inquired about life in his native land. But, the longer David has lived in the United States, the more reluctant he has become to identify himself as Jamaican. Uncle Cameron identifies himself as American when he chooses. David struggles daily with the temptation to enter fully into American life, thus weakening his ties to his Jamaican heritage. Would it bring more acceptance? From whom?

Rather than discovering prejudice, David has found life at FSU and in Conway almost too accommodating. Because Conway is open to people of different ethnic origins, David is not seen as unusual and is viewed by the citizens as just another international college student. On the other hand, this positive view is not necessarily helpful to David, as he struggles with maintaining his Jamaican heritage.

As a social worker, you will practice in communities that appear to place a strong emphasis on particular ethnic or racial customs and traditions, **cultural pluralism**. In these communities, the festivals, parades, and gatherings help people to remain connected to their racial and ethnic roots.

Other communities may dictate uniformity in behaviors and customs based on the prevailing (often white) norms and values of the community. This is known as **Anglo-conformity**. In these communities, people from other countries have few opportunities to celebrate their heritage and country of origin other than within their immediate families.

Still other communities attempt to combine the cultural and ethnic uniqueness of the people who reside in a location into one distinctly new entity: a **melting pot**. In this environment, ethnic and racial backgrounds are deemphasized in favor of unity and community wholeness.

At first glance, David appears to be experiencing the community as a melting pot. While this initially appears to be a positive community attribute, David's living circumstances relate directly to reevaluating his self-concept.

Sentiments toward people from foreign nations vary according to nation of origin (Herring, 1993). Because David is from Jamaica would you anticipate any unique community-based difficulties or advantages in the future? As a social worker, you will need to be sensitive to the community's response to an immigrant group.

Finally, what opportunities exist in Conway for David to connect with his Jamaican upbringing? Are there international organizations at FSU or other resources in neighboring communities that would provide avenues for David to maintain his Jamaican heritage?

Societal Level

What is the general perception that American people have of Jamaicans? How much accurate information do U.S. citizens possess about these persons? In our society, exposure to Jamaica for many people has been limited to the Jamaican bobsled team, the movie *Cool Runnings*, Red Stripe beer, Jamaican rum, news accounts of Jamaican drug rings, or vacation tales from Caribbean tourists. While David has been fortunate, during his stay in the States, to avoid stereotypes associated with Jamaican males, this might not always be the case.

What were David's expectations on coming to America? Did he believe all Americans were rich and self-centered or altruistic and privileged? Was David's perception of people from the United States distorted by limited contacts with American tourists and by media?

Perhaps some Americans, upon learning that David is from Jamaica, wonder if he is involved in illegal drugs. Meanwhile, other Americans might hold prejudicial views questioning the work ethic of a Jamaican male. In order to refrain from stereotypes, it is important to attempt to gain understanding of how people in our society view David and how he perceives people in his new environment.

The social worker should also be familiar with special policies, laws, or rules governing a Jamaican student's stay in the United States. Toward this end, the U.S. Immigration Service or U.S. congressional offices might be able to assist in identifying any special provisions or requirements that regulate academic study by Jamaicans in the United States.

Finally, the social worker should explore the existence of any national organizations that focus on Jamaica or the needs of Jamaicans in the United States. While national Jamaican associations may not have a local chapter in the FSU area, such organizations could broker information to Jamaicans across the United States or serve to network Jamaicans regionally via newsletters, computer bulletin boards, or referral services.

International Level

David's situation is well suited for a discussion of international issues in social work practice. First, David reminds us of the many people living in the United States who have emigrated here from other countries. Indeed, America is a nation of people from other countries. Mindful that our clients often originate from diverse backgrounds in a global sense, social workers need to become "world wise" in their approaches to the client-worker situation. Each client who has grown up in a different culture represents a new journey and adventure in assessment for the social worker.

Jamaica is a country whose economic health relies heavily on bauxite and sugar exports as well as on tourism. During the early 1980s the Reagan administration attempted to strengthen a weakened Jamaican economy by making it a model of a free market society. The strategy was to increase Jamaica's foreign aid from the United States to over $495 million a year, double the amount given in previous years (Braun, 1991, p. 70). This monetary infusion, however, had little impact on the wage scale of Jamaicans (with minimum wage below $9 per week) and resulted in few new jobs while creating a windfall profit for investors and entrepreneurs. This is an example of how the wealthy prosper and the common citizens benefit little from foreign aid.

David comes from a strong, working-class family that failed to experience any positive impact from the economic policies initiated in the 1980s by the United States in Jamaica. Indeed, David's presence in the United States is a testimony to a combination of his family's determination, the political contacts nurtured by his mother, and the willingness of Uncle Cameron to provide support for David while he is living in the United States. From the perspective of David's family and country, he is clearly obligated to return to Jamaica following completion of his degree.

As social workers, what do we know about immigration laws and research describing trends in transnational migration that may impact David (Massey, Goldring, and Durand, 1994)? Juanita, David's girlfriend, is a U.S. citizen. David's rights concerning citizenship and his visa are topics for assessment. If they were to marry, would Juanita be allowed to return with David to Jamaica or could David apply for U.S. citizenship? Ultimately, for David to make an informed decision as to where to live, he needs to understand his choices and their consequences. The answers to some of David's questions involve both immigration law and differing customs between the two nations.

APPLYING A SOCIAL WORK FRAMEWORK: VALUE-CONFLICT THEORY

Earlier in this chapter, basic tenets of a value-conflict perspective were examined. Social policies and programs were viewed as products of special interest groups competing with each other for limited resources. From this perspective, what is deemed legitimate or illegitimate is a result of particular groups successfully exerting dominance and influence over the interests of other groups.

For David, the values and positions forwarded by special interest groups and systems are also important elements. For example, David's family and country have firm expectations that David will return to Jamaica. However, David's girlfriend, his uncle, the community in which David now lives, and the university he attends are supportive of his staying in America.

Various constituencies in the United States continually compete to define the rights and expectations of immigrants. Recent legislation in California aimed at prohibiting aid to illegal immigrants and their children is a product of this kind of effort. Some political groups oppose state and federal aid to immigrants because of the financial obligations and consequences of such support. Other religious or social welfare groups favor aid to immigrants for altruistic reasons.

In part, David's future is shaped by groups of people who organize to promote their vested interests. It is important for David and his social worker to ascertain which groups have the greatest potential impact on this young man's situation and what level of advocacy is appropriate to assist him in attaining his goals.

SUGGESTED ACTIVITIES

1. Most universities sponsor an international student coalition. Seek information concerning this organization and plan to attend some of their cultural events and programs. Become familiar with the special needs of international students at your school.

2. Attempt to visit or vacation in a foreign country. If this is not feasible, attend a travel show or exposition focusing on a country you hope to visit. Strive to gain an appreciation of the culture, values, norms, and ways of people in this country.

3. Attend a political or special interest group meeting or rally. Ask for brochures, pamphlets, and literature describing the group's positions on important social issues. Inquire about politicians or media personalities who champion the group's cause.

REFERENCES

Berry, M. (1992). An Evaluation of Family Preservation Services. *Social Work*, 37(4), 314-321.

Braun, D. (1991). *The Rich Get Richer*. Chicago: Nelson-Hall.

Cowley, G. (1994). The Culture of Prozac. *Newsweek*, February 7, 41-42.

DiNitto, D. (1995). *Social Welfare: Politics and Public Policy*. Boston: Allyn and Bacon.

Federico, R. (1990). *Social Welfare in Today's World*. New York: McGraw-Hill Book Company.

Hardert, R., Gordon, L., Laner, M., & Reader, M. (1984). *Confronting Social Problems*. St. Paul: West Publishing Company.

Herring, C. (1993). Ethnic Notions about Alien Nations: American Ethnic Groups' Changing Sentiments toward Foreign Nations. *Sociological Focus*, 26(4), 315-332.

Jacobsen, J. (1994). Trends in Work Force Sex Segregation. *Social Science Quarterly*, 75(1), 204-211.

Kilbourne, B., England, P., & Beron, K. (1994). Effects of Individual, Occupational, and Industrial Characteristics on Earnings: Intersections of Race and Gender. *Social Forces*, 72(4), 1149-1176.

Lidz, T. (1976). *The Person*. New York: Basic Books, Inc.

Longres, J. (1995). *Human Behavior and the Social Environment*. Itasca, IL: F.E. Peacock Publishers.

Lowery, D., & Gray, V. (1994). Do Lobbying Regulations Influence Lobbying Registrations? *Social Science Quarterly*, 75(2), 382-384.

Marmor, T. (1973). *The Politics of Medicare*. Chicago: Aldine Publishing Company.

Massey, D., Goldring, L., & Durand, J. (1994). Continuities in Transnational Migration: An Analysis of Nineteen Mexican Communities. *American Journal of Sociology*, 99(6), 1492-1533.

McDonell, J. (1993). Judgments of Personal Responsibility for HIV Infection: An Attributional Analysis. *Social Work*, 38(4), 403-410.

McKee, M., & Robertson, I. (1975). *Social Problems*. New York: Random House.

Palmer, E., & Little, G. (1993). The Plight of Blacks in America Today. *Social Behavior and Personality*, 21(4), 313–325.

Papalia, D., & Olds, S. (1989). *Human Development*. New York: McGraw-Hill Book Company.

Rosenbaum, E. (1994). The Constraints on Minority Housing Choices, New York City 1978–1987. *Social Forces*, 72(3), 725–747.

South, S., & Deane, G. (1993). Race and Residential Mobility: Individual Determinants and Structural Constraints. *Social Forces,* 72(1), 147–167.

Stolzenberg, R. (1994). Educational Continuation by College Graduates. *American Journal of Sociology*, 99(4), 1042–1077.

Trent, K. (1994). Family Context and Adolescents' Expectations about Marriage, Fertility, and Nonmarital Childbearing. *Social Science Quarterly*, 75(2), 319–339.

Vannoy-Hiller, D., & Philliber, W. (1989). *Equal Partners: Successful Women in Marriage*. Newbury Park, CA: Sage Publications.

Western, B. (1994). Unionization and Labor Market Institutions in Advanced Capitalism, 1950–1985. *American Journal of Sociology*, 99(5), 1314–1341.

Wong, Y., Garfinkel, I., & McLanahan, S. (1993). Single-Mother Families in Eight Counties: Economic Status and Social Policy. *Social Service Review*, 67(2), 177–197.

Zastrow, C., & Kirst-Ashman, K. (1990). *Understanding Human Behavior in the Social Environment*. Chicago: Nelson-Hall.

7

Middle Adulthood

In this chapter we examine the macro issues of middle adulthood and focus upon the role of the social worker as facilitator during this turbulent passage. The midlife dreams of many men and women focus on personal achievement. There is something exciting about entrepreneurs, inventors, and entertainers who have "made it big." The success of a Bill Gates, Colin Powell, Ted Turner, or an Oprah Winfrey confirms the American dream. We see them as persons who began with few resources but through hard work and determination became rich and famous.

Professional athletes often seem to emerge quickly from relative obscurity to stardom. Who has not heard of Michael Jordan, Martina Navratilova, or Wayne Gretzky? Their names are symbols of success to many American children and adults. Yet, their celebrity status is often gained at great cost. Athletes, like others trying to succeed, struggle to balance various roles and responsibilities as spouse, parent, daughter, or son while pursuing life ambitions. To become a renowned athlete requires an extensive commitment of time and energy.

A highly recognized professional golfer, Lee Trevino is now in his late fifties and a star on the Senior PGA Tour. Known

to most Americans as the "SuperMex," he has been the winner of the 1968 U.S. Open, three Canadian Opens, two PGA Championships, two British Opens, and numerous other PGA and Senior PGA tournaments (Trevino, 1982). Elected to both the PGA and World Golf Halls of Fame, he is known in the sports world for his illustrious golf play and for a positive, cheerful demeanor.

Life for Lee Trevino has not always been gratifying. Born into a family of migrant workers in Texas, Trevino used apples for golf balls and invented putting games around his grandfather's shack (Gilbert, 1992, p. 31). As a child, Trevino learned the game of golf with an old discarded five iron. Later, as a caddie at Glen

Lakes Country Club, Trevino would become a fierce competitor, acquiring golf prowess by playing against other caddies on three small holes located behind the caddie shed (Gilbert, 1992). Trevino's self-taught, unorthodox golf swing, hard work ethic, and passion for golf have become his trademarks. He challenges young golf pros by demanding, "The sun's up. Why aren't you playing golf?" (Gilbert, 1992, p. 40). His daily routine has focused almost exclusively on golf, but he has also promoted his public image with advertisements and related business ventures.

Lee Trevino's love for golf over the past decades has not diminished but other aspects of his life have changed. Following a hole-in-one at a nationally televised "Skins Game" during the early 1990s, a surprised course announcer, expecting to hear a thrilling description of the amazing shot, instead heard Trevino suggest that golf was not everything. Trevino implied that two previous marriages and his relationships with his adult children had been impaired by a lust for golf and the insatiable demands of the sport.

Now in middle age, and establishing a family with his third wife, Trevino frequently expresses a desire to spend more time with his family. Those who follow the Senior PGA Tour know that many of the older, more seasoned players are changing their lifestyles and work patterns. They are looking for ways to better accommodate their family obligations and to gain greater satisfaction in relationships with family members and friends. This involves reducing playing schedules, inviting their children to caddie for them, bringing family and friends to tournaments, and other innovative plans.

For a professional athlete, the expectations surrounding practice and play, meeting with media, entertaining sponsors, product endorsements, and involvement in charitable work can be overwhelming. Individually, athletes might diminish these demands by cutting back on their work-related activities but they risk the reputation of having diminished commitment to the game. Another solution by senior players is to intentionally reduce actual work expectations.

For the social worker, knowing how to balance personal and professional time becomes a necessary skill. For example, some employers of social workers expect volunteer hours although compensation is based on a 40-hour work week. Various flexible time arrangements that restructure employment to address both agency needs and personal responsibilities have been implemented in recent years. These variants on the traditional work schedule often meet the needs of both client and worker.

THEORY: ROLE

Role theory is a helpful perspective as we view macro issues of the middle years. Role theorists frequently quote this well-known passage from Shakespeare's *As You Like It* (act 2, scene 7):

All the world's a stage,
And all the men and women merely players:
They have their exits and their entrances;
And one man in his time plays many parts,...

The analogy of actors on a stage and role-players in society can be very useful. This **dramaturgical approach** provides a means to assess individual behaviors in relationship to social structure. Role theory has become so prominent that it "has become part of the very web of social work thinking and literature" (Strean, 1967, p.77).

Just as actors learn and perform clearly defined parts from written scripts, people in real life acquire various statuses and roles that dictate behavioral conformity and adherence to social norms. In much the same way as actors perform parts as villains and heroes, people act out roles as student, worker, friend, spouse, and parent. Each role involves social expectations that define how to behave, think, and feel. As role-players, we must adapt our lives to bosses, teachers, and other persons who occupy positions of power over us. Rather than playing to audiences, people in real life respond to the situation and those around them.

A **role theory perspective** requires that:

> Individuals in society occupy positions, and their role performance in these positions is determined by social norms, demands, and rules; by the role performances of others in their respective positions; by those who observe and react to the performance; and by the individual's particular capabilities and personality. The social "script" may be as constraining as that of a play, but it frequently allows more options. (Biddle and Thomas, 1966, p. 4)

For role theorists, the social script is defined predominantly by the expectations and behaviors of others. From the standpoint that the social script is powerful and demands conformity, role theory reflects social determinism. While individuals occupying positions and playing roles may be viewed as having different role-playing skills and capabilities, heavy emphasis is placed on social conformity and the power of those with whom one interacts.

One notable contrast to role theory's social-deterministic ways involves Goffman's (1959) emphasis on individual control in his book *The Presentation of Self in Everyday Life*. Although clearly using a structural approach, he gives added attention to how "the individual may deeply involve his ego in his identification with a particular part, establishment, and group." Through analysis of concepts like "impression management," Goffman explores individual interpretation and control over "the presentation of self" in social roles (1959, p. 243).

The concept of role is the point of articulation between society and the individual. While recognizing that much debate exists over a clear and concise definition of social role, Turner offers three basic conceptualizations:

> **Prescribed Roles.** When conceptual emphasis is placed upon the expectations of individuals in statuses, then the social world is assumed to be composed of relatively clear-cut prescriptions. The individual's self and role-play-

ing skills are then seen as operating to meet such prescriptions, with the result that analytical emphasis is
drawn to the degree of conformity to the demands of a
particular status.

Subjective Roles. Since all expectations are mediated
through the prism of self, they are subject to interpretations by individuals in statuses. When conceptual emphasis falls upon the perceptions and interpretations of
expectations, then the social world is conceived to be
structured in terms of individuals' subjective assessments
of the interaction situation. Thus, conceptual emphasis is
placed upon the interpersonal style of individuals who
interpret and then adjust to expectations.

Enacted Role. Ultimately, expectations and the subjective assessment by individuals of these expectations are
revealed in behavior. When conceptual priority is given to
overt behavior, then the social world is viewed as a network of interrelated behaviors. The more the conceptual
emphasis is placed upon overt role enactment, the less
analytical attention to the analysis of either expectations
or individual interpretations... (Turner, 1974, pp. 165–166)

While considerable attention is given to how individuals
actualize roles in a given script, less attention is given to how
various social scripts can develop and change. Persons can alter
expectations and rules governing their behavior.

DEVELOPMENTAL ISSUES

Social scientists refer to middle age as a time of reflection and
self-evaluation. Prompted by physical changes and the realization that one's life is half completed, people at middle age
begin to review. What have I already accomplished? What have
I left undone? What are priorities in my life?

The term "midlife crisis" characterizes the struggle of people from their late thirties to middle sixties as they react to a
perceived "time squeeze" (Friedan, 1993). How do I achieve all
that remains important to me in the time left? Sometimes feel-

ing as if they have lived their lives for others, middle-agers often proclaim that "it is time to start doing what I want to do," as they chart new directions. Others see this as a time to turn away from egocentric pursuits and to begin to focus their efforts more on contributions to the welfare of the community.

Using a role-theory perspective, we find that middle age is a prime time for evaluating social roles (worker, father/mother, husband/wife, daughter/son), role salience or importance, and one's commitment to roles as well as to the norms and rules that oversee each. Our focus in this chapter is twofold: emphasizing **role shifts or adjustments experienced during middle age** and **the impact of changing social scripts for role enactment during middle age**.

Multiple role involvement, characteristic of our society, is often labeled as a negative—time-consuming and mentally draining. Yet, Gilbert (1988) and others suggest that the opposite may be true. When an individual embraces multiple roles, her or his identity transcends any single role. When this is the case, if a person forfeits or vacates any single role through job loss, divorce, childlessness, retirement, or even illness, other roles are available to contribute to self-definition.

Conversely, when people invest heavily in a single role (e.g., worker or parent) but later relinquish this role, either voluntarily or involuntarily, loss of identity may occur. Understandably, this void may be psychologically and emotionally devastating. John Updike's (1960) story of a middle-aged man who lives in the tarnished glory of his high school basketball days is told in *Rabbit, Run*. Although he was a husband, father, son, and employee, Rabbit's energy and role identification had ossified his psychological growth at an adolescent marker. In the interest of growth and psychic health during middle age, it is wise not to invest all one's energy in a single role.

Gender Differences

Life experiences differ for males and females during middle adulthood. While there are increasing opportunities and choices available to women during middle age, equitable roles between women and men in the worlds of both work and family still do not exist (Gilbert, 1993, p. 106).

We know, for example, that women and men enter different kinds of occupations and that women continue to earn significantly less than men in the labor force (United Nations, 1991). The needs of husbands and children continue as major concerns for women who are employed (Moen, 1991). Although husbands and fathers are assuming a more equal share of home chores and child care, a careful look reveals that employed women still take primary responsibility for work in the home. Research also indicates that middle-aged women are disproportionately called upon to provide care to older parents (Brody and Schoonover, 1986).

These examples reflect larger societal views defining the scripts and roles played by women and men during middle adulthood. Women of middle years, like other women in the United States, live in a male-dominated society. While societal norms concerning a "woman's place" are changing, how middle-aged women perceive, weigh, and enact various social roles is influenced by their social position and their community.

Is it reasonable to expect a middle-aged man to change jobs and move to a new area to accommodate a spouse's career move? Men often point out the impracticalities of giving up their jobs to support a wife's occupational pursuits. "We will lose money! How would we live? Why would you want to do that? Can't you be satisfied just raising a family?"

However, women are expected to make such adjustments. Changing employment for males may be seen as best for the family, a step up the ladder regardless of any other considerations. Traditionally, women have been asked to give husbands' jobs priority regardless of the investment they have in their own positions. It is assumed that the wife can seek another job. The implication is that the husband's career is more important.

As we begin to explore the performance of various roles during middle age, consider the impact of gender as well as other sources of power on social scripts and role expectations.

Are there differing standards and rules for various individuals in the United States? Do some groups of people exert greater control over social roles and scripts than others? Is it easier in middle adulthood to define and determine one's own life direction? To the extent that predominantly white, male professionals can modify their job conditions, is it reasonable to assume others can?

Women at Middle Age

Current literature has created an overemphasis on the negative aspects of middle age for women.

> The middle years for women are often described as the worst—as a time of adolescent children, crises, suicides, the departure of husbands, empty nests, fading charms, melancholia, responsibilities for aging parents, and pressures to prepare for financial security in their final years. In addition, there are all sorts of physical reminders that one is not as young as one used to be, such as wrinkles, weight gain, menopause, and screenings for breast and uterine cancers. (Hunter and Sundel, 1994, p.114)

This negative account of midlife women is one-dimensional. As a remedy, a more balanced perspective describing both limitations and opportunities for women in middle age is needed. While recognizing the existence of emotional ups and downs for women during midlife, let's see the glass as half full rather than half empty.

Middle age is not by definition necessarily a time of crisis, turbulent change, or calamity. Research by Spitze and Logan (1990), for example, suggests that actual time spent performing duties—juggling of full-time work, interactive marriage, active parenting, and helping parents—may not be unduly burdensome. For example, in instances where women care for both their parents and children in the home, older children have been found to serve important supportive functions for women (Raphael and Schlesinger, 1994).

Approaching this time period for females from a positive perspective, midlife can be a time of self-actualization, characterized by new and exciting opportunities and challenges. Peterson and Klohnen (1995) observe that women in midlife are likely to become politically active. Their findings suggest that "expressions of generativity are not limited to family or work life but are manifested as well in concerns for the wider national and international spheres" (Peterson and Klohnen, 1995, pp. 27–28). Thus, middle-aged women may seek opportunities for new roles.

ROLE OF PARTNER OR WIFE Divorce for people of middle age in the United States is common. Years ago those who divorced were stigmatized and were viewed as irresponsible or immoral. In recent years, however, divorce has become acceptable. Ultimately, the availability of divorce provides women with additional choices and increased freedom. Still, the strong emphasis on family values and monogamous marriages, and the desire of courts as well as religious and community groups to see children reared in two-parent families, tends to undergird traditional role assignments.

Bogolub (1991, p. 428) describes the typical dilemmas faced by women who are divorced in middle age as "loss of a long-held position, the possibility of over-dependence on young adult children, a shrinking remarriage pool, socially denigrated body changes, and unfair labor market conditions." While Bogolub recognizes the need for women to reframe divorce as a challenge to growth on an individual basis, she does not communicate a clear sense of the abilities of women experiencing divorce to create and sustain close links with other adults.

In minimizing the harmful effects of divorce, Hunter and Sundel (1994) propose that midlife can constitute an opportunity for women to redevelop intimate relationships with partners. Liberated from worry over pregnancy, they can acknowledge sexual interest and enjoyment. With children out of the home, women also feel a new sense of freedom and control over their lives. In a positive sense, marital relationships and their role expectations can facilitate expansion, renegotiation, and redefinition in middle age.

On the other hand, the decreased income that frequently accompanies divorce cancels out advantages anticipated by those who see rosy possibilities in the single life. The costs of child care, support of family, and adequate housing are economic realities. Both income and status often go down for women, while men—especially those who do not meet child support payments—fare somewhat better.

Women do not march to the beat of a single drum. A variety of relational paths are available to them in middle age. Some restructure relationships with husbands; others decide to stay single but be sexually active. Still others choose other women as romantic and sexual partners (Gilbert, 1993). The traditional assumption that all middle-aged women eventually either become passive, depressed wives or assume "divorcee" roles is both outdated and sexist. Social workers can empower women to make both micro- and macro-level choices that result in satisfying relationships.

PARENTING The focus of much attention concerning women and middle age relates to the "empty nest" syndrome. Following menopause and the departure of children from the home, some women express depression and despair. Yet, many eagerly await the day their children leave the home. As offspring become more independent and move away, they require less parental time, energy, and resources. Now mothers can gain further control over their lives and seek new interests and activities as they rechannel energy into work, education, the arts, and volunteerism.

The stereotype of a middle-aged housewife sitting at home forlorn and bewildered by the emotional void and idle time produced by the "empty nest" is overstated, if not misleading. Many women welcome the opportunity to develop alternatives or engage in new roles at the completion of child rearing. Freed of parenting responsibilities, women in middle adulthood can more easily concentrate on defining and developing themselves.

In *The Fountain of Age* (1993), Betty Friedan recounts her Outward Bound wilderness survival expedition at the age of 60. Finding resources deep within herself, her identity unknown by the group, she emerged from the experience with heightened awareness of new spiritual, mental, and physical strength, realizing she could play the old games or could experience new adventures in work and love.

OCCUPATIONAL ROLE Current and future financial status is a major concern for women in middle age. The threat of poverty for older women is both profound and severe (Hunter and Sundel, 1994). In large part, fear of poverty can be attributed to reliance on husbands for financial security. Women who face divorce or widowhood but lack employment experience are at greatest risk. Early work experience may be helpful in middle age.

Expectations relative to middle-aged women and employment are changing. Now many women welcome the opportunity to work outside the home and view their careers as an important source of their identity (Barnett, Biener, and Baruch, 1987). The benefits of middle age may include an increased opportunity to develop "professionally and to have established a sense of self separate from a man and children, economic independence, and perhaps greater intellectual companionship and contentment" (Gilbert, 1993, pp. 111–112).

However, for this group to attain self-actualization through participation in the labor force, discrimination in employment based on age and sex must be eliminated. These women often rely upon temporary, "dead end," or sex-segregated jobs—such as unskilled secretarial and retail sales positions—for employment (Weitzman, 1988).

Women in the mid-years bring valuable knowledge and skills to the workforce, even when they have limited prior employment experience. But, much like actors who become typecast in particular roles, many find themselves trapped in jobs that limit their progress and fail to provide challenges. Upgrading and acquiring strategic skills to obtain better paying occupations becomes a necessity. And attaining these skills requires advocacy for policies and legislation that challenge corporate America to rewrite the social script and assure middle-aged women fair access to higher-status positions.

THE PARENTAL CARETAKER ROLE Who cares for older parents in need? The answer is women. "This patriarchal society officially recognizes the social need to *care about* children and the elderly by assigning women to *care for* them" (Sancier and Mapp, 1992, p. 63). It is frequently expected that women should be able to undertake a combination of homemaking, a job, and care of an aged parent—a challenging, if not unrealistic, association of roles.

When middle-aged daughters are asked to take primary responsibility for their elderly parents, they do so with difficulty and sacrifice. Typically, daughters help with such tasks as shopping, transportation, and emotional support. They are also likely to become involved with cooking and personal care for their parents (Brody and Schoonover, 1986). A daughter may also be expected to adjust her job to meet parental needs.

Middle-aged women in these circumstances struggle for balance. How can they manage home, work, and caregiving? Overburdened by conflicting demands of work and family, such a woman is like an actor asked to play too many roles in an overly demanding, emotionally draining drama.

The long-term resolution to this dilemma, however, does not lie in encouraging or enabling middle-aged women to do more. The broad issue of dependent care by daughters is a gender issue that demands solutions. "Women should become leaders in finding solutions that are woman friendly" (Sancier and Mapp, 1992, pp. 62–76).

But does this place another demand upon those who already are overburdened? Perhaps corporate America, with its preponderance of men in leadership roles, should assume this onerous responsibility. Redefining the care of older parents as societal, family, and workplace responsibilities is required.

Men also need to serve as caretakers. Currently, when men address the needs of others it is viewed as an expression of compassion; for women it constitutes an expected duty (Sancier and Mapp, 1992). By what unwritten law were women assigned to— and men excused from—serving as parental caretakers? Governments and employers should consider "family-friendly" policies that enable both men and women to address the needs of elderly parents. Family leave legislation and policy should be amended to include explicit language concerning the care of older parents by their adult children.

Middle-Aged Men

Because of the uneven balance of socioeconomic power between men and women, men are able to be more selective with regard to participation in basic roles: marriage, work, and the care of dependents. As seen daily in the workplace, men exert greater influence than women in defining social scripts and in the enactment of roles.

We do not suggest that middle adulthood is uneventful for men. In this life stage they experience divorce, career changes, and the redefining of relationships with children and parents. New relationships are traumatic and life changing for men as well as for women. A major difference, however, is that men often have more resources to effect role changes.

Predominantly white, middle-aged men are the investors, writers, producers, and directors in the drama of life in America. Scripts and roles are developed to serve the purposes and desires of those in power, and when this does not occur the scripts are rewritten or recast.

Many employers in the United States have established affirmative action policies for hiring. Frequently, affirmative action officers implement and monitor these practices. It is interesting, however, to view the employment process when executive-level positions such as chief executive officers, vice presidents, and general managers are selected.

Often, company presidents and boards of trustees create special rules for executive-level hires. The rules are often cloaked in a spirit of urgency and secrecy requiring immediate action. Since there is an assumption that few people are qualified for such major positions, decisions are made "confidentially." In these "special cases," the affirmative action officer may be informed by the board or president of the intent to circumvent normal hiring practices. In fact, such exceptions are often explicitly authorized in an affirmative action policy manual. The result is that the president hires "his man" and the "good old boy" system remains intact. Women as well as other minorities identify in this system a well-polished and maintained glass ceiling.

Those who have followed affirmative action employment guidelines over the years understand the closed door discourse in these situations. The justification for such decisions may include: "We have known and respected Jeffrey for years, and we know he is a good man." "I hear he is ready for a change, especially since his recent divorce." "This promotion would provide Jeffrey with new opportunities in a different city, and he's someone we can count on!"

Like those who can influence the casting of prime parts in productions, men have traditionally helped each other by making a few phone calls to important people involved in hiring processes. They are also known to provide buddies with opportune introductions to assist in their job hunting. Men who have developed various connections over the years are in a position to call in favors to assist in their midlife transitions and those of their associates. Conversely, women who divorce in middle age often have fewer influential contacts and must approach the process as if they are starting over (Hayes, Anderson, and Blau, 1993, p. 104).

While men can claim certain advantages from role changes in middle adulthood, following divorce they do not fare as well in their relationships with adult children. Findings by Cooney and Uhlenberg indicate:

> Divorce has a pronounced negative effect on the frequency of men's contacts with their adult offspring, significantly reduces the likelihood that men have an adult child in their household, and sharply reduces the proba-

bility that fathers consider their adult children as potential sources of support in times of need. (1990, p. 677)

While middle-aged men may find change relatively easy, the consequences in relationships with their children may be profound. Although middle-aged men in our society appear capable of generating appreciable influence over the definition and enactment of various social roles, after divorce they may find it hard to maintain satisfactory contact with the children, especially after remarriage.

Gay Men and Lesbian Women: Middle Age and Parenthood

Homosexuals face many forms of institutional and social discrimination both with family members and at work. However, in middle age many people make a last attempt at parenthood. This can be a special concern for gays and lesbians as from an "institutional perspective, same-sex couples and individual homosexuals do not have the same civil and legal rights as do heterosexuals" (Depoy and Noble, 1992, p. 49). Parenthood is a role our society has been unwilling to accord to gays and lesbians.

In middle age, everything you see appears in a different light. Fathers and sons included. In middle age, not only do you hear Time's winged chariot hurrying near, you also catch the shrill ring of that biological alarm clock mentioned in articles about women wondering if they should have children before it's too late. It rings, I suspect, with decreasing volume, for the rest of one's life. But it never quite stops. If, as Carlyle wrote, the answer to life is either **Yes** or **No**, then the answer to "Will I have children?" is equally stark. There are no in-betweens: nieces, nephews, friends' children can be pleasures, but no answer… So you wanna have a baby? I know gay men who have had children and are very proud of them; gay men who are ashamed of theirs (because they left their children, after the divorce which followed their coming out); gay men thrilled to be not associated with kids; and gay men patiently walking their dogs through Washington

Square who think deep down that the one thing that would have made them happiest in life is—children. (Holleran, 1989, p. 3)

One of the more depressing aspects of stage life for any actor involves lead roles never played. Knowing that one could have played the part, but was never cast for it, is disheartening.

Many of us acknowledge that discrimination, whether a result of sexual orientation, gender, race, socioeconomic status, or any combination of elements, is a powerful force in American culture. For middle-aged persons, it may be a harsh realization that discrimination was the basis for never acquiring one or more of the desirable lead roles in life.

CASE EXAMPLE

Mrs. Pamela Stern is employed as a social worker at the Western Hills Office of Mental Health Services, Inc. (MHSI). Located in the western suburbs of a large metropolitan city, the Western Hills office offers a wide range of community mental health and family services.

Several years ago, two utility companies, a clothing retail group, and a large department store chain began a contractual arrangement with MHSI to address problems faced by employees: family issues, day care, worker alienation, mental health, substance abuse, and retirement planning. Following the program's success, fifteen other companies and businesses have established agreements with MHSI for employee assistance services.

Pamela's caseload is evenly divided between referrals from the community and contracted businesses. Her major responsibility involves intervention with individuals and families.

Mrs. Jean Royer, a 53-year-old employee of the department store chain that is in the contract group, approached Pamela for help. Jean has had over 15 years' experience with the company, first as a secretary and later as a clerical supervisor. Recently, as the result of a restructuring of personnel in the company, Jean was promoted to support staff manager at their regional corporate headquarters.

Given a small monetary increase and a new title, Jean originally was pleased with her promotion. The leap from an hourly job to a more prestigious position—with a salary increase at this stage of life—was exciting. Soon, however, Jean became discouraged with her work situation and how it had altered her life.

Jean recently discovered that the company is engaged in a 12-month plan aimed at "right sizing" the labor force. One element of the plan is a 15 percent reduction in the secretarial staff. This change is to be accomplished by arranging secretaries into centralized secretarial pools, one of which Jean administers.

Now a part of management, Jean feels overwhelmed with company secretarial demands. The workload created by laying off 15 percent of the secretaries is excessive. Jean averages 50- to 55-hour work weeks as she continues to do her part in the secretarial pool. Because she is now a salaried employee, her male superiors expect her to shoulder responsibility for job completion in secretarial services. When approached about the situation, Jean's boss stated, "Welcome to management. You will have to learn how to handle long days and nights."

Jean's relationship with her husband, Fred, began to suffer as a direct result of her promotion. The couple is contributing toward their son's college tuition and board. While her small pay increase is useful, Jean is more interested in having time with Fred and in seeking new hobbies, interests, and relationships. Jean finds that her excessive hours affect quantity and quality of time spent with Fred. While originally supportive of Jean's promotion, Fred has expressed increasing frustration over the new position.

TIME TO THINK!

As a social worker at MHSI, Pamela performs several professional roles. She is an individual and family therapist as well as a consultant and advocate for planned change in organizations.

For funding, MHSI depends heavily upon service contract arrangements with local businesses in the community. Given the agency's financial reliance and the presenting situation, what ethical considerations emerge for Pamela in assessing macro-level systems? Can Pamela be objective in her assessment of Jean's presenting situation, knowing that Jean's employer constitutes an important MHSI contract? Is being a female social worker an advantage or disadvantage for Pamela?

MACRO SYSTEMS, MIDDLE ADULTHOOD, AND GENDER

As you have likely surmised, a major premise in this chapter is that midlife experiences for women and men are significantly different. Considering organizational, community, societal, and global factors, examine the relevance of gender in this case example. Would males find themselves in this kind of dilemma? Why or why not?

Organizational Level

Because of her tenure with the company, Jean has expressed an interest in exploring change from within the system rather than resigning her position. Pamela has collected information describing the organization's structure, job descriptions, employment policies, and procedures, as well as employee rights as described in the department store's newly revised personnel manual. As the department store is nonunion, a labor relations specialist is available through MHSI to assist in assessing procedural and legal aspects involved in realigning the department store's labor force.

Over the years, Jean has been troubled by the demeaning manner in which women are viewed and treated in the company. Expectations of long work hours are often accompanied by low pay and minimal recognition of individual skills or needs. Many company officials see women in supportive positions as secretaries, cleaning persons, and food-service workers, but rarely in leadership roles. Indeed, Jean's promotion confirmed her perceptions when it became apparent that support staff managers possessed little power and were not invited to attend management meetings or functions.

Unfortunately, these attitudes can apparently be traced to the founder of the company. Although he will soon retire, the heir apparent, his son, may not have a more enlightened view of the role of women in the company. This is cause for concern, since nearly all of the current executives are men.

Community Level

The client in this example lives in the western suburbs of a Great Lakes city. Once a thriving, heavy-industry and automobile manufacturing center, the city's economy has suffered greatly as a result of decreased production in the manufacturing sector.

The downtown area of this city has been decimated by business failures. Plagued by high unemployment and crime, many major businesses and stores have moved to the suburbs for survival. However, even there, opportunities for people seeking long-term employment are very limited. In many instances, employers can select employees from a large and stable labor pool. Those who have steady employment are made to feel fortunate.

Jean and other employees have heard rumors that the department store might relocate its regional corporate headquarters to another city, but the recent office reorganization suggests that these reports, for the time being, are inaccurate.

Employment opportunities for women around the city are primarily service and clerical or staff support positions. Additionally, the marketplace for these openings is highly competitive. If Jean were to leave the department store and pursue another job in the community, she would likely lose credit for her years of experience and find it necessary to accept a lower-paying, less prestigious position.

A recent survey funded by Working Women, a local advocacy group, confirms a high degree of worker alienation among women in the area. The department store chain appears to treat female employees the same way as do other employers in the city.

Societal Level

When changes occur in employment and earnings because of recessions and the loss of manufacturing jobs, such as those experienced in the now famous "rust belt" of the United States, women often seek and assume stronger economic roles (Zippay, 1994). As they take on a greater share of the financial support of their families, women often feel trapped into taking and maintaining jobs that are unfulfilling and represent underemployment (Briar, 1988). Particularly in times of economic downturn, women feel pressured to take positions with little power and limited opportunity for advancement.

Nationally, businesses are driven by the dual goals of increasing earnings and survival. Fierce competition exists between department store chains in the United States. Corporate managers in this field are granted promotions and bonuses for devising less costly ways of producing greater revenue. Increased profit motive with little concern for human rights and fairness has become a norm.

In order to cut costs, department stores have learned to rely heavily on a disposable labor force of low-paid employees. Except at the very top of the corporate ladder, long-term commitment and loyalty to a company have given way to cost containment strategies.

Middle-aged women are particularly vulnerable to employment exploitation. Like many other women in America, Jean senses that she is unappreciated and feels manipulated by her bosses. Quitting would only allow the company to hire a younger, less experienced, and lower-paid person as her replacement. It would be a difficult challenge after age 50 to find employment with equal benefits.

International Level

Several important international themes appear in this case example. International trade and industry have affected the client system in several distinct ways. The loss of jobs and commerce in automobile-related industries—a result of the success of foreign imports—has clearly contributed to the economic downturn in this Great Lakes city. Employers know jobs are scarce and take full advantage, in their hiring and employment practices, of the deluge of applicants.

Competition among department store chains has also been fueled by foreign rivalry. The introduction of "hypermarkets" by international investors has created a revolution in the industry. By hiring low-cost workers, the hypermarket stores have forced American competitors to rethink employee relations and methods for delivering service. On more than one occasion, Jean has been told that, given the competitive nature of the marketplace, restructuring the regional office is necessary for economic survival.

"Gender bias in occupational distribution and pay is also a worldwide phenomenon" (Nichols-Casebolt, Krysik, and Hermann-Currie, 1994). The labor of women is exploited throughout the globe. In order to undercut prices, companies in less-developed countries often pay women and children shockingly low wages to produce products for American markets. While women in industrialized regions have not been adequately involved in business decisions, women in developing countries have few, if any, rights with regard to shaping their roles in employment.

APPLYING A SOCIAL WORK FRAMEWORK: ROLE THEORY

We began this chapter with an examination of life changes for senior professional golfers and the way in which they are exerting control over expectations on the professional golf tour. Using role theory, an analogy was drawn between life and the stage. People were viewed as actors in a play, each performing parts written in social scripts.

In the case example, role theory was the underlying theme used to identify factors influencing the creation of a workplace script and the enactment of occupational and family roles. Unlike male professional golfers, Pamela's client struggles with power and control in defining her work environment.

As an actor on a stage, Jean finds herself cast in a role created and interpreted by male directors. Several unique factors have given store executives freedom and options to write, cast, and direct this department store drama. A male-oriented business, a city experiencing economic decline, and employment needs in a highly competitive industry present a challenging plot to be resolved. Feeling powerless, Jean seeks ways to alter the organizational pattern that defines her role and those of her coworkers.

In this situation, Pamela plays a vital part. As an agent of change in a contract-for-service agency, she must approach problems with an awareness of a multitude of systems, including the individual, family, organization, community, and society. Attending to immediate needs, Pamela has initiated both individual and family intervention for Jean. However, because Pamela has established a close and trusting relationship with Jean and also has the respect of business leaders who contract for MHSI services, she is well positioned to suggest ways that will reshape Jean's role in the company. Each of these strategies is an important consideration, but as we focus on macro changes, let us look at what Pamela may be able to do.

Several macro issues are apparent to Pamela as she repeatedly hears female employees complain of oppressive working conditions. Women are routinely subjected to subservient work roles and scripts written and produced by men. Lack of flexibility in the work arena produces severe psychological stress and family dysfunction and requires attention through policy formation/development and social legislation.

At a macro level, Pamela will explore the feasibility of a flexible time program and will introduce a team decision-making model at Jean's workplace. Pamela is also on the planning committee for a local Women and Work Conference. She has asked Jean to organize a workshop to examine dilemmas experienced by women in entry-level management positions.

Garvin and Tropman stress that "coalition building, establishing networks, developing data bases, and engaging in various kinds of public relations and societal information activities set the stage for societal change and become an important component of it" (1992, p. 205). Pamela is committed to individual and family intervention as well as to seeking ways to resolve differences between her client and business leaders at the department store chain. She is committed to working with her clients in groups and individually to explore ways to eliminate sexism, ageism, worker alienation, and other forms of oppression against middle-aged women in the marketplace.

SUGGESTED ACTIVITIES

1. Many professors and university administrators are middle-aged. As a class, examine the leadership positions at your school in relationship to gender. What percentage of full professors are women? Identify factors contributing to the ratio of women to men in these positions.

2. Develop a class debate. Argue the merits of the "bring your daughter to work day" in order to sensitize girls to work roles.

3. Organize a meeting or forum examining the virtues of middle age. Structure the event to emphasize positive changes that middle-aged people have made both individually and as a group.

REFERENCES

Barnett, R., Biener, L., & Baruch, G. (1987). *Gender and Stress.* New York: The Free Press.

Biddle, B., & Thomas, E. (1966). *Role Theory: Concepts and Research.* New York: John Wiley and Sons, Inc.

Bogolub, E. (1991). Women and Mid-life Divorce: Some Practice Issues. *Social Work,* 36(5), 428-433.

Briar, K. (1988). *Social Work and the Unemployed.* Silver Spring, MD: National Association of Social Workers.

Brody, E., & Schoonover, C. (1986). Patterns of Parental Care When Adult Daughters Work and When They Do Not. *The Gerontologist,* 26, 372-381.

Cooney, T., & Uhlenberg, P. (1990). The Role of Divorce in Men's Relations with Their Adult Children after Mid-life. *Journal of Marriage and the Family,* 52, 677-688.

DePoy, E., & Noble, S. (1992). The Structure of Lesbian Relationships in Response to Oppression. *Affilia,* 7(4), 49-64.

Friedan, B. (1993). *The Fountain of Age.* New York: Simon and Schuster.

Garvin, C., & Tropman, J. (1992). *Social Work in Contemporary Society.* Englewood Cliffs, NJ: Prentice-Hall.

Gilbert, L. (1988). *Sharing It All: The Rewards and Struggles of Two-career Families.* New York: Plenum.

Gilbert, L. (1993). Women in Midlife: Current Theoretical Perspectives and Research. In N. Davis, E. Cole, & E. Rothblum (Eds.), *Faces of Women and Aging.* New York: The Hawthorne Press.

Gilbert, T. (1992). *Hispanics of Achievement: Lee Trevino.* New York: Chelsea House Publishers.

Goffman, E. (1959). *The Presentation of Self in Everyday Life.* Garden City, NY: Doubleday Anchor Books.

Hayes, C., Anderson, D., & Blau, M. (1993). A Startling Report on Women and Divorce. *Ladies' Home Journal,* 110(5), 98-106.

Holleran, A. (1989). Time's Scythe. *Christopher Street,* 5, 3-5.

Hunter, S., & Sundel, M. (1994). Midlife for Women: A New Perspective. *Affilia,* 9(2), 113-128.

Moen, P. (1991). Transitions in Mid-life: Women's Work and Family Roles in the 1970s. *Journal of Marriage and the Family*, 53, 135–150.

Nichols-Casebolt, A., Krysik, J., & Hermann-Currie, R. (1994). The Povertization of Women: A Global Phenomenon. *Affilia*, 9(1), 9–29.

Peterson, B., & Klohnen, E. (1995). Realization of Generativity in Two Samples of Women at Midlife. *Psychology and Aging*, 10(1), 20–29.

Raphael, D., & Schlesinger, B. (1994). Women in the Sandwich Generation: Do Adult Children Living at Home Help? *Journal of Women and Aging*, 6(1/2), 21–45.

Sancier, B., & Mapp, P. (1992). Who Helps Working Women Care for the Young and the Old? *Affilia*, 7(2), 61–76.

Spitze, G., & Logan, J. (1990). More Evidence on Women (and Men) in the Middle. *Research on Aging*, 12(2), 182–198.

Strean, H. (1967). Role Theory, Role Models, and Casework: Review of Literature and Practice Applications. *Social Work*, 12(2), 77–87.

Trevino, L. (1982). *They Call Me SuperMex*. New York: Random House.

Turner, J. (1974). *The Structure of Sociological Theory*. Homewood, IL: The Dorsey Press.

United Nations (1991). *The Women's World 1970–1990*. Trends and Statistics.

Updike, J. (1960). *Rabbit, Run*. New York: Knopf.

Weitzman, L. (1988). Women and Children Last: The Social and Economic Consequences of Divorce Law Reforms. In S. Dornbush & M. Strober (Eds.), *Feminism, Children, and the New Families*. New York: Guilford Press.

Zippay, A. (1994). The Role of Working-Class Women in a Changing Economy. *Affilia*, 9(1), 30–44.

CHAPTER

8

Later Adulthood

Tools in hand, roof tiles tucked under his arm, the retired chief executive of the nation startled America as he clambered over roof peaks. As a volunteer builder of homes for the poor this man has modeled the use of resources and skills of the older adult.

Former President Jimmy Carter epitomizes the potential and integrity of America's seniors. The media continue to picture President Carter and his wife, Rosalynn, as hands-on builders for Habitat for Humanity and as ambassadors negotiating peace in troubled areas of the globe.

In dedicating his book of poems, *Always a Reckoning* (1995), Jimmy Carter reveals the roots of his post–White House activities:

> To my mother, Lillian, who never let racial segregation, loss of loved ones, ravages of age, or any other principalities or powers stop her sharing what she had or was with the least of those she knew…

We begin this chapter with the present Jimmy Carter rather than the President Jimmy Carter. In the image of his mother, James Earl Carter has refused to be defined as inept and "over the hill." To the disappointment of Carter detractors,

he refuses to be relegated to the shadows in his later years. Although no longer the leader of our nation, Jimmy Carter rejects the premise that a retired person loses a sense of worth.

Now, as a former president and senior citizen, Jimmy Carter is known for his peacemaking activities in such troubled sites as Central America, North Korea, Haiti, and Bosnia. He has become a college professor and author and is deeply involved in policy analysis at the Carter Center. He is respected internationally for his peacemaking and humanitarian efforts. Some suggest that Jimmy Carter should be recognized as the United States' most outstanding president. His social consciousness has also made him a serious contender for the Nobel Peace Prize (Jaynes, 1995).

In many respects, Jimmy and Rosalynn Carter feel fortunate. In *Everything to Gain: Making the Most of the Rest of Your Life*, their co-authored book, they state,

> What we had come to realize as "retired" people is that
> we have a lot more leeway than ever before to choose

our own path, to establish our own priorities. We had a lifetime of training and experiences on which to base these decisions, and our financial resources would be adequate to meet our needs. We had nothing to lose in whatever we did and everything to gain. (1987, p. 33)

These words come from a one-term First Family that was crushed upon losing their reelection bid to Ronald Reagan. Rosalynn Carter recalled, "There was no way I could understand our defeat. It didn't seem fair that everything we had hoped for, all our plans and dreams for the country could have been gone when the votes were counted on Election Day" (1987, p. 9).

After losing the election they could have left the White House and returned to Plains, Georgia, to live in isolation and bitterness. Instead, the Carters refocused their energies. They became involved by helping others both domestically and internationally.

As exemplified by the presidential couple, older age can be a time for growth, new adventures, and making a difference in the lives of others. When wisdom and experience are used in voluntary service, older people often gain a newfound sense of enrichment and self-worth. Schools, libraries, hospitals, social service agencies, businesses, and other community organizations benefit from the helping hand of senior citizens in America.

Older adults often struggle with their place in our society. They are led to believe that their time and competency have passed. However, the resources of older adults are underused in the United States. Active community and societal participation by senior citizens not only contributes to our nation, but enables seniors to maintain personal competencies and acquire social power.

How the story of a peanut farmer from Georgia ends and how he is remembered are yet to be determined. However, how Jimmy Carter wishes to be thought of is clear.

In "A Committee of Scholars Describe the Future Without Me," Jimmy Carter wrote,

Some shy professors, forced to write
about a time that's bound to come
when my earthly life is done
described my ultimate demise
in lovely euphemistic words
invoking pleasant visions of
burial rites, with undertakers,
friends, kinfolks, and pious pastors
gathered round my flowery casket
eyes uplifted
breaking new semantic ground
by not just saying
I have passed on
joined my maker
or gone to the Promised Land
but stating the lamented fact
in the best and gentlest terms
that I, now dead, have recently
reduced my level of participation. (1995)*

THEORY: SOCIAL RECONSTRUCTION

So far we have selected and applied general sociological theories to each developmental time period. However, in this chapter we describe **social reconstruction theory**, an orientation specific to older age.

The basic tenets of social reconstruction theory are found in Kuypers and Bengston's (1973, p. 182) analysis of social breakdown and competence in older age. They suggest that, as a result of social reorganization that occurs in later life, older people are devalued and develop negative self-images.

---

*From ALWAYS A RECKONING AND OTHER POEMS by Jimmy Carter. Reprinted by permission of Times Books, a division of Random House, Inc.

Older adults typically experience the loss of occupational roles and established social networks. As this loss occurs, they receive feedback from others that they are less needed and less valued. In this way, older persons are stripped of their dignity and opportunities to productively use knowledge and abilities they have spent a lifetime developing.

Rice defines social reconstruction theory as "a theory of aging describing how society reduces the self-concept of the aged, and proposing ways to reverse this negative cycle" (1995, p. 635). He identifies the following four steps:

1. *Our society brings about role loss,* offers only sparse normative information and guidance, and deprives the elderly of reference groups, so that they lose the sense of who they are and what their roles are.
2. *Society then labels them negatively* as incompetent and deficient.
3. *Society deprives them of opportunities* to use their skills, which atrophy in the process.
4. *The aged accept the external labeling,* identify themselves as inadequate, and begin to act as they are expected to act, setting the stage for another spiral.

While most sociological theories provide only an analytical framework for gaining insight about social phenomena, social reconstruction theory proposes three considerations to help end social breakdown during older age. Kuypers and Bengston (1973, pp. 194–198) suggest that on a macro level society members should reflect upon:

1. **Defining personal competence as successful role performance.** A person's worth in our society is disproportionately weighted in relationship to one's performance in economically productive roles—work. When an older person retires, self-worth suffers. What alternatives exist for defining personal worth? While recognizing that a shift in values is no simple task, greater emphasis on wisdom, experience, creativity, and volunteerism as a personal basis for assigning worth would benefit older adults.

2. **Defining competency in terms of capacity to adapt to change.** Various helping professions have a rich tradition of providing clinical services to assist older people in adapting to environmental change. However, the competency of older adults should not be judged solely on their ability to adapt and to provide for themselves. When society helps assure adequate health care, housing, and financial security, senior citizens are freed to pursue personal meaning and expression in later life, as in the case of Jimmy and Rosalynn Carter.

3. **The ability of older adults to exert control.** People in older age are susceptible to losing control over their lives. Senior citizens must be empowered to be decision makers regarding the social policies and programs that affect them and their positions in life. Self-worth in older age can be directly equated to the ability to maintain power and engage in self-determination.

To summarize, social reconstruction theory provides social workers with a perspective for assessing planned change at the societal level that will benefit older adults. These general themes include focusing on ways to: reduce the importance of work and encourage alternative activities as sources of self-worth; promote societal responsibility for health care, housing, financial status, and other social services for older adults; and empower senior citizens to establish self-rule.

DEVELOPMENTAL ISSUES

Old age is viewed negatively and stigmatized by many in our society. Loss of independence, physical health, sexual appetite, activity level, employment, and financial security are reported in the literature as common problems for senior citizens.

Ageism—that is, prejudice against the elderly—continues to be experienced by a high proportion of those over 65. It may take the form of discrimination or bias in employment situations, forced retirement of the elderly, substandard care in nursing homes, or restrictive attitudes toward sexuality. When society limits the elderly to subsistence and maintenance goals, it contributes to a negative view of this age group.

Beryl Williamson, a 75-year-old ice skating instructor at Michigan State University, believes her age was a factor that kept her contract from being renewed. Though there is no required retirement age for contracted employees, she will be replaced after 43 years of teaching. Her income will drop $12,000 without the contract renewal (Pena, 1996).

Sensitivity and interest concerning issues confronting people in older age have risen over the years as the numbers of senior citizens in our society have increased. The U.S. Bureau of Census estimates that by the year 2000, 13 percent of the population in the United States will be over 65 years of age (Cox, 1993, p. 3). It is important to note that in this aging society more people are living healthier and longer lives than ever before. Sixty-five is not a benchmark for physical or mental decline.

Business leaders and government officials have learned to appreciate the over-65 group as vital constituents. When senior citizens organizations like the American Association of Retired Persons (AARP) speak, business leaders and politicians now listen. AARP has over 250 publications, covering a multitude of topics including consumer information, finances, health, and personal planning, that inform members about important issues. Senior citizens constitute a powerful force in our society, united like no other age group.

Since 1950 there has been a White House Conference on Aging approximately every ten years. These have been used to inform government leaders of the needs of seniors. During the Reagan and Bush administrations, there was limited if any expansion of social service policies and no 1990 White House Conference on Aging (Cox, 1993, p. 315).

As noted earlier, our review of macro-level developmental issues for later life is guided by social reconstruction theory. Consequently, the literature presented focuses on mechanisms for enhancing the image and integrity of older adults, as opposed to a description of the various physical and mental problems encountered during older age (Hancock, 1990).

Senior Citizens as Volunteers

As with Jimmy and Rosalynn Carter, senior citizens in general represent an inestimable resource for community and national service in the United States. Research by Gallagher (1994) indicates that when compared to younger adults, seniors do their fair share in volunteering time, particularly to the needy. Gallagher suggests that older adults help others in numerous ways, whether by providing emotional support during crises, giving sustenance, or assisting people in their daily trials and tribulations. Assisting relatives, as well as more familiarized volunteering, was found to be an important element in the lives of many older adults, especially older women.

Gallagher's findings refute the common belief that older adults disengage from social relationships and caring for others. Instead, "When it comes to hours of volunteering, specifically volunteering to help the needy, older men and women actually spend more time than do their younger counterparts, even when controlling for employment status" (Gallagher, 1994, p. 576). As health and energy permit, senior citizens are a rich source of volunteer assistance in many communities.

Many factors have to be considered, however, when using volunteers: ageism, racism, and sexism. Morrow-Howell, Lott, and Ozawa, for example, caution social workers that for senior citizens, while "race itself does not affect volunteer helping behavior…higher levels of contact and client satisfaction are reported when the volunteer and the client are of the same race" (1990, p. 395). They suggest that problems associated with using older adults as volunteers, including the impact of race, can be effectively addressed by professional instruction and support.

When social workers do more than "troubleshoot" but also give professional training and supervision to elderly volunteers, they help provide structure, purpose, support, recognition, and meaning to volunteer activities. Seniors better serve others, and probably experience greater satisfaction, when social workers make a concerned effort to match volunteer with client and services rendered. A major role for social workers in these instances is to produce "successes." Successes are defined as effective delivery of volunteer services, enhancing the self-worth and integrity of the volunteer.

Just as President Clinton used Jimmy Carter's expertise to help establish peace in Haiti, social workers maximize the potential for success by utilizing volunteers' strengths. Perkins and Tice (1995) remind us that older adults and clients share an important common thread: they are survivors. Both yearn for control and independence in daily living. Social workers must become stockholders in volunteerism, continually assessing ways to build upon strengths and to enhance the value of clients, volunteers, and the helping enterprise.

To optimize successes and retain elderly volunteers, Fischer and Schaffer provide five important suggestions.

1. Selective recruitment, or matching volunteers with appropriate assignments and screening out people who are likely to be uncommitted volunteers....
2. Careful monitoring of new volunteers can help avert the post-honeymoon blues effect during the first few months of volunteering.
3. To maintain the commitment of volunteers, it is important to offer intrinsic rewards—that is, jobs that are challenging, interesting, and important.
4. A critical factor in sustaining the commitment of volunteers is to provide for successful experiences.
5. Friendship is an important factor in volunteer commitment. (1993, p. 205)

While older adults should be thought of as potential volunteers in various ways, a growing body of research demonstrates their usefulness with regard to peer education and counseling. Shannon and colleagues (1983), for example, found success in recruiting and training older adults as peer educators in a nutrition-awareness program. Similarly, Hoffman (1983) described her program for peer counseling with the elderly. Goodman (1984) reported the merits of the "helper bank" in which older people enter reciprocal arrangements to assist each other.

Given the involvement of the elderly in volunteering, one wonders why senior citizens are not more adequately acknowledged and rewarded for their activities. The successful Retired Senior Volunteer Program (RSVP), active in most large communities, provides a model for appreciating seniors while society benefits from well-structured services. Better recognition of their efforts could be instrumental in reshaping the image of senior citizens from dependent recipients of care to healthy and involved persons.

Unfortunately, older adult volunteers are rarely viewed as having an integral position in society. Is this because volunteer work, compared to paid employment, is not highly valued? Are people expected to become volunteers simply because they have extra time?

Three perspectives identified in the literature suggest why seniors should volunteer. Using these views, it is important to pay special attention to how older people are depicted. Is there an emphasis, explicit or implied, on work-role loss? How are older people characterized or stigmatized with regard to their skills and capabilities? Are older volunteers viewed with dignity or as "has-beens"?

The **inoculation perspective** suggests that keeping active (and doing good) is "good" for the elderly; that is, older people who are active are happier and healthier than older people who are withdrawn or "disengaged." Thus volunteer work can inoculate, or protect, the older person from the hazards of retirement, physical decline, and inactivity.

The **debit perspective** reflects a contemporary economic concern—that older people are a drain on society, that the elderly have received special privileges and benefits from policies and programs based on age rather than need, and that there are too many of them.... Thus, when older persons serve...they potentially are reducing the drain on public funds from other elderly in need.

The third perspective, the **leisure perspective**, is different from the other two. This perspective defines volunteerism as a form of leisure activity. Retired persons, under this rubric, are consumers. Volunteer work is their choice; if it is enjoyable and meaningful to them, then maybe they will choose to participate in volunteer activities. (Fischer and Schaffer, 1993, pp. 3-11)

These orientations are disturbing and problematic as they depict public opinion of older adults and volunteerism. From the inoculation perspective, emphasis is not placed on the contributions of elderly volunteers, but volunteerism is cast as an activity primarily benefiting seniors. From the debit perspective, "the idea that older persons have a special debt to society to compensate for the burdens they are imposing is ethically troublesome" (Fischer and Schaffer, 1993, p. 10). Finally, the leisure perspective gives no credence to "the special nature of volunteers service and suggests that volunteerism is no more (or not much more) important than playing bridge or tennis, in terms of its social impact" (Fischer and Schaffer, 1993, p. 11).

Older adults who volunteer deserve respect and credit for their humanitarian efforts. To facilitate such recognition, the AARP constructed a "Bill of Rights" in 1985 for senior volunteers. The AARP promotes these principles and encourages their dissemination to older volunteers.

BILL OF RIGHTS

The Right to be treated as a co-worker—not just free help.

The Right to suitable assignment—with consideration for personal preference, temperament, life experience, education and employment background.

The Right to know as much about the organization as possible—its policies, people, and programs.

The Right to training for the job and continuing education on the job—including training for greater responsibility.

The Right to sound guidance and direction.

The Right to a place to work—an orderly, designated place that is conductive to work and worthy of the job to be done.

The Right to promotion and a variety of experiences through advancement or transfer, or through special assignments.

The Right to be heard—to feel free to make suggestions, to have a part in planning.

The Right to recognition—in the form of promotion and awards, through day-by-day expressions of appreciation, and by being treated as a bona fide co-worker. (American Association of Retired Persons, 1985, p. 15)

Finally, Chambre (1984) poses an extremely salient but multidimensional question. Is it reasonable to conceptualize volunteering as a relief for role loss in older age?

Chambre suggests that people who have maintained an active level of participation in the labor force up to retirement do not seek volunteer activities to regain the prestige of a paid job. Instead, the writer proposes that "elderly volunteers may be volunteers who became elderly; that is, their involvement is a continuation of behavior patterns established earlier in life" (1984, p. 297).

While their prominence in volunteerism accentuates the integrity of senior citizens as a group, America is a country dedicated to paid work, not just work. Volunteerism is commendable but not revered. Therefore, seniors also need to consider ways to promote other aspects of their worth, including, but not limited to, humanitarianism.

Senior Citizens and Work

The advertisement reads "Highly experienced worker seeks part-time employment. Open to learning on the job, flexible concerning hours, willing to work for reasonable compensation." This notice could appear in any daily newspaper. Senior citizens represent a plethora of knowledge and experience for the labor force, accompanied by a willingness to be productive. Are there positions for these older, often retired persons, in the marketplace? If so, how can older people find employment that matches their interests and backgrounds?

At a macro level, Morris and Bass suggest a role for higher education.

1. Urban and metropolitan elderly populations, although characterized predominantly by limited income and education, have the interest and capacity to perform socially useful and significant tasks in their retirement.
2. A university can provide a concentrated period of competency building which will equip interested elders to perform complex and significant tasks and to fill new and significant service or decision-making roles in their communities.
3. The university can develop a liaison and active coalition with nonprofit civic groups and public authorities to ensure that a mechanism exists for moving from competency acquisition into significant community roles. (1986, p. 16)

Collaboration between senior citizens and universities has many merits. Elderhostel, an educational adventure for older adults, is a shining example of such mutuality. A nonprofit educational organization, it offers inexpensive, short-term academic programs hosted by educational institutions around the world. Recent data indicate more than 250,000 persons enroll annually in these programs offered in the United States and throughout the world (Dade, 1994).

The eager return of many older adults to the classroom indicates a readiness for educational growth. At the same time, these seniors share their life experiences and maturity with students and faculty. Participants often return to their neighborhoods eager to volunteer with their newly acquired skills.

Such older adults may be placed in prominent positions that contribute to their higher esteem in peer groups.

Social workers need to explore projects and programs that successfully link older adults to the labor force—beyond volunteerism and rudimentary service-oriented employment. Many senior citizens are willing to work part-time or to trade wages for a modest reimbursement for expenses, for the sake of maintaining a desirable status and making occasional use of their experience and background.

In our aging society, older adults face widely different socioeconomic circumstances. Some will struggle to remain in the primary marketplace through full-time employment as long as possible. Others, associated with progressive companies and corporations, will benefit from part-time work, consulting, or post-retirement roles. Still others will emphasize their leisure interests in retirement.

As suggested by Morris and Bass (1986), one macro-oriented strategy worthy of consideration is the expansion of the marketplace. Stimulation of the economy that creates new businesses and jobs produces opportunities for all Americans. These efforts would assist interested seniors in finding satisfying and valued work roles.

Locally and nationally, social workers have also contributed to the development of a secondary economy, where special needs and social objectives not met in the primary economy are addressed by senior citizens. Through participation in programs such as the Peace Corps, Foster Grandparents, RSVP, Meals-on-Wheels, and Second Harvest capabilities of seniors outside their career skills may be utilized, with little or modest remuneration or compensation as found in the traditional workforce.

Political Activism in Old Age

Traditionally, the elderly have been thought of as a strong political force in America. In addition to the AARP, senior citizen organizations including the National Council of Senior Citizens, the Gray Panthers, and Save Our Security have been influential fact-finding and lobbying entities (Quadagno, 1991). As publisher of *Modern Maturity* with the third highest circulation in the nation, the AARP has repeatedly demonstrated its political clout. The "gray lobby" has given older adults sociopolitical stature and guided age-related public policy formation and development in the United States.

However, Day (1993) suggests that assessing the impact of elderly constituents and interest groups on the aging policy process is difficult and complex. She identifies three divergent views of older people with regard to political activism.

1. Grey peril—where senior citizens are seen as a formidable political group of "greedy geezers" out to bargain for more than their due of community and societal resources.
2. Fading grey—where senior organizations are seen as losing power and influence and becoming increasingly ineffective with regard to protecting existing benefits and raising new issues and policies.
3. A progressive view—where older adults promote broad-minded change aimed at intergenerational unity and promoting a comprehensive and compassionate social welfare system. (Day, 1993, p. 426)

Some will argue that a growing population of older Americans, characterized by a propensity for voting and demanding favors from politicians, supports a gray peril view of older adults in the political arena. Seniors have the numbers and know they have clout, and government officials are frightened of their power (*The Economist*, 1989).

Others will contend that senior citizens are prone to support a liberal government agenda. They emphasize that older adults view government intervention as an important mechanism for addressing societal ills. Indeed, *Modern Maturity* (1995) reports that 35 percent of senior citizens believe the best way to halt declining values in America comes through strengthening both governmental and individual responsibility.

McKenzie (1993), however, provides an interesting argument supporting the fading gray perspective. He predicts that federal expenditures for programs for the elderly will be curtailed and may actually fall gradually as the turn of the century draws near. His contention is based on a perceived reduction in the political power of senior citizens.

McKenzie gives eight reasons "that the sheer growth in elderly numbers and population share will undercut, albeit marginally, the political influence that elderly interest groups and lobbies have on Congress":

- There is a "free rider" problem, where many older Americans are seen as sitting back and assuming that others will do the lion's share of work to maintain political influence.

- The cost of mobilizing large numbers of elderly will outdistance the number of elderly, depressing their desire to engage in political activism.

- Senior citizens are growing more diverse with regard to their political objectives.

- Younger people are increasing their political effectiveness.

- Nonelderly political groups are raising objections to the growth in a perceived "Elderly Welfare State."

- Older adults are continuing to work beyond the typical retirement years with working seniors separating themselves from political efforts of their retired counterparts.

- Wealthier senior citizens are being taxed more, thus producing another division in the senior citizen voting bloc.

- New small groups representing well-defined public and special interests (e.g., AIDS, education, or anti-crime) will better compete with the elderly for political influence. (McKenzie, 1993, pp. 75–76)

In assessing the "big picture" with respect to the position of older adults in the American scene, social workers must carefully consider McKenzie's premises. Political activism and clout are important to senior citizens for maintaining and improving economic, social, and health services. Stated another way, a vital key to self-rule and integrity of the elderly in our society is their ability to influence the politicians who formulate and execute the policies and programs that affect them. A formidable body of research (e.g., Storey, 1986; Blackburn and Chilman, 1987; Gist, 1992; Meyer and Bartolomei-Hill, 1994) has emerged describing the nature of current and proposed legislative and budgetary changes that attack the quality of life for senior citizens. The common theme warns of an erosion of benefits for aged individuals, whether through policy changes, program reductions, or tax reform. While the impact of these cuts would be felt by all senior citizens, the most severely affected are the elderly at or near poverty-level incomes, single women, and the frail elderly.

McKenzie identifies specific areas where Congress has begun to reduce benefits which should constitute concerns for the elderly now and in the future.

- Raising age requirements for full retirement from age 65 to 67.
- Modifying calculating schemes that reduce the real purchasing power of social security benefits.
- Increasing the taxability of social security benefits.
- Decreasing real Medicare costs covered by federal insurance, accompanied by increases in Medicare premiums.
- Changing the measure of cost of living by the Bureau of Labor Statistics. (1993, p. 80)

Empowering Those in Older Age

Social workers concerned about macro-level issues during older age must assess various venues for social empowerment. **Empowerment** involves helping individuals or groups of individuals to gain power (Staples, 1990). Social workers who have senior citizen clients need to look at the full range of ways to allow seniors to function on their own behalf.

A beginning step involves dispelling the myths that contaminate and cloud our perception of older adults in America. Senior citizens are frequently portrayed as inactive, depressed, ill, unattractive, asexual, set in their ways, demented, unable to learn new ways, or withdrawn (Harrigan and Farmer, 1992). These stereotypes are powerful and undermine the image of older adults in America; social workers should seek to discourage such falsehoods. It is also important for social workers to engage seniors in social policy discourse and the acceptance of responsibilities. Remembering the client-centered nature of social work practice, social workers facilitate policy activity until client leadership emerges. As clients define concerns and policy priorities, social workers become partners with them in social policy analysis and practice (Cox and Parsons, 1994, pp. 64–65). To assist social workers, Cox and Parsons identify the following five empowerment-oriented tasks:

1. Overcoming workers' and clients' resistance to involvement in the policy process.
2. Obtaining and sharing information regarding existing policies, pending policies, and implementation of policies.
3. Gaining and sharing knowledge about the policy process and policy makers.
4. Developing and testing frameworks for understanding and analyzing policy.
5. Acquiring and sharing practical knowledge about how to change policy. (1994, p. 64)

While each of the five tasks is difficult to implement, overcoming resistance to involvement is a prerequisite for addressing the remaining four. Seniors often feel in danger of losing control over their lives. Others appear to be making more and more decisions for them. The elderly, as a population at risk, often feel powerless in solving their own problems. First and foremost, social workers need to reassure seniors that as a group they are a political force and can reclaim control of their lives.

Once convinced that social change is possible, older adults are free to explore their shared concerns about issues such as housing, work, health care, income, and transportation. The Older Americans Act (OAA) of 1965 opened doors, set national objectives, and established mechanisms through Area-wide Agencies on Aging (AAA) that legitimized the ability of older Americans to pursue their rights. Social workers need to be aware of planning organizations like the AAA in the regions in which they practice. It is vital that they be familiar with the diverse policy and legislative opportunities that will advance concerns of their clients (Hancock, 1990, p. 234).

Looking Ahead

On a positive note, Cox states,

> If the values of the twenty-first century shift along the lines suggested by the social scientists, we should expect an improvement in the status of older persons. Less emphasis on achievement and productivity, in which the young are always viewed as having the greatest potential for development, and greater concern with interpersonal relationships and the meaning and quality of life, in which the old may have the distinct advantage of breadth of experience and wisdom accumulated over a lifetime, should improve the status of older persons. (1993, p. 344)

Older adults are currently confronted with various social perils, including retirement, role loss, age discrimination, negative stereotyping, and dependency. Our commitment is to ensure that future social policies and services are designed to build upon the strengths of seniors and enrich their lives (Cox and Parsons, 1994, p. 28). As with all forms of macro-level assessment, "the social worker's primary responsibility is to clients.... The social worker should make every effort to foster maximum self-determination on the part of clients" (National Association of Social Workers, 1990, p. 1).

CASE EXAMPLE

Mrs. Carla Peters is a social worker at the Timberland Senior Citizens Center. Located in a middle-class section of a city (population 200,000) in the northwestern United States, TImberland offers a wide range of services for older adults. These include health and nutrition programs, an activities program, individual counseling, a peer companion and phone network, and the presentation of various seminars and workshops.

One of Carla's favorite roles is coordinating Timberland's "Pulse and Power Program" (PPP). Created three years ago in response to concerns over Medicare reductions, the PPP meets weekly to examine and address important local and national issues affecting the elderly. The PPP publishes a monthly newsletter which is sent to all patrons of Timberland. Normally, 30 to 35 older adults attend meetings with a leadership council composed of seven members elected annually. The vast majority of members are lifelong residents of the community.

Recently, the PPP has focused on a highly controversial local issue. The county park's wildlife refuge and petting zoo may soon be forced to close or curtail services. This would affect all citizens—the young, school-age children, families, as well as seniors. A county budget crunch, coupled with an electorate reluctant to pass new tax millage, has prompted politicians to consider closing the 50-year-old wildlife facility.

At the last PPP meeting, seniors were very vocal. They identified two areas for exploration in connection with saving the wildlife center. First, how could PPP members and others at Timberland effectively lend political support for the county wildlife program? Second, the PPP leadership committee and Carla were asked to assess the possibility of establishing a formal relationship with the wildlife refuge and petting zoo in order to utilize senior volunteers. This association might free personnel and resources at the refuge for other functions. Additionally, a link between the senior citizen center and the wildlife center would have political advantages for the next park levy.

PPP members wanted to become guides and resource people at the wildlife refuge and petting zoo. After formal training by park officials, senior citizens envisioned greeting visitors and being stationed throughout the park to provide educational information concerning various birds, animals, and plant life, and their natural habitats in the region. Several PPP members have expressed an interest in wearing uniforms that represent the timber industry's rich heritage in the area. Others were excited at the prospect of designing and creating authentic Timberland garb.

Carla sensed the great enthusiasm among the elderly. Thinking about ways to support the animal refuge center was meaningful and important for senior citizens. Many older adults viewed participation at the refuge center as an opportunity to share their knowledge of nature and the community and to interact with younger people. Members were encouraged because park administrators and county politicians have also shown interest in exploring this association.

With the park levy due to reappear on the ballot in nine months, Carla saw ideal timing for exploring a formalized linkage between the highly motivated senior citizens and the park services. The park system would benefit by acquiring valuable resources and political support. In addition to individual gains, Carla felt that senior citizens would enhance their image as active doers in the community.

TIME TO THINK!

Carla's client in this example is the senior group at the Timberland Senior Citizens Center. While she is interested in their personal growth and development, on a macro level Carla also works to break down common societal beliefs that older Americans are deficient or incompetent.

Along with the PPP leadership committee, Carla has been charged to examine the merits of a formal association with the county park system, with a focus on the animal refuge center and petting zoo. What factors are important for Carla to consider in assessing this situation? How can Carla best orchestrate this process, remembering the social worker's obligation to foster client self-determination? How is social power an important factor in discussions with park system officials?

MACRO SYSTEMS AND OLDER ADULTS

Social workers whose practice includes older adults need to evaluate their actions in relationship to both micro and macro systems. Assessing macro systems, like micro systems, is a client-centered process that links client and social worker in partnership. With this perspective, assess and identify important organizational, community, societal, and international factors in creating a program that relates senior citizens to a county animal refuge center. As you do this, maintaining and developing self-rule and integrity for senior citizens should be priorities. You must avoid the tendency to stereotype and place limits on how seniors are expected to act and function.

Organizational Level

As PPP members and Carla began to examine the primary organizations involved, two different organizational models became apparent. What initially seemed to be a simple idea for an association between two entities now appears more complex.

Although receiving federal, state, and county funds, Timberland Senior Citizens Center is characterized by professional leadership, a high degree of consumer participation, and flexibility. Timberland's Board of Trustees, most of whom are older adults themselves, maintains and exerts direct control over policy and program development. Timberland's executive director has a positive, professional relationship with the Board of Trustees. The director has informed the Board regarding the prospect of an association with the park system and has received strong support.

Conversely, the county park system is more bureaucratic and political. The park system is strongly influenced by both national and state policy. Because of the hierarchical authority structure of park personnel, any agreement between Timberland Senior Citizens Center and the park relative to volunteering at the wildlife refuge and petting zoo must be approved by the chief park officer. In addition, legal counsel representing the park system must evaluate any proposal to ascertain its merits, since there are county, state, and federal mandates.

Both organizations favor the concept of older adults volunteering at the refuge center. However, the differences between Timberland's professional model of organization and the park system's public model cause both to approach program implementation very differently. Timberland's Board can make decisions and carry out plans in a timely manner, whereas park officials are bound to rules of procedure. As an example, Timberland Senior Citizens Center promptly offered its van for transporting senior citizens to and from the park. Meanwhile park officials struggled with the feasibility of expanding current job descriptions to include training and support of seniors as volunteers in the park.

Members of the PPP leadership committee, however, did not stand by waiting to see if their support for the refuge center died in bureaucratic red tape. Based upon their knowledge and experiences over the years, several seniors have developed important alliances with county commissioners as well as state politicians. Being careful to coordinate their contacts with Timberland and park officials, several seniors made phone calls to assess ways to assist the chief park officer and his staff in bringing this program to fruition. Indeed, over the years, Carla has carefully noted the resourcefulness of senior citizens in identifying influential individuals in key organizations that provide help.

Community Level

Timberland Senior Citizens Center is located in a community experiencing little new economic growth. Although it was once a major timber-producing area, employment in the community now relies on four small manufacturing companies. The economic climate in the community has changed little during the past decade. More than 18 percent of the population is over 65 years of age.

Senior citizens in the area are politically active. They vote, they participate in political parties and movements, and a few older adults hold key political offices, including that of mayor. Even though they do not typically vote as a bloc along party lines, older adults can become highly organized on community issues that they regard as in their best interest. Thus senior citizens comprise an important political group for shaping the future of the park system as well as for passing a park levy. One of the more disturbing aspects of the community involves the segregated nature of housing for older adults. Most seniors live in "Old Pine Town," the name given to the older, center section of the city developed during the timber industry's most prosperous years. While the senior center has worked to help create a transportation system making the community more accessible to the elderly, many older adults continue to feel isolated. Transportation is an important factor in fulfilling the hopes of those senior citizens who desire to participate at the refuge center. By volunteering at the park, older adults not only interact with different age groups, but potentially enhance their image and stature with children and families.

Interestingly, local newspapers and television have provided positive coverage concerning the possibility of a senior citizen–wildlife refuge affiliation. Seniors are being cast in the community as protectors of animals, heritage, and family activities. While being sensitive not to upstage the efforts of politicians and park officials, senior citizens gain pride from community approval.

At the request of the PPP leadership committee and Timberland's executive director, Carla has also contacted the AAA for their support of the wildlife refuge endeavor. In the past, the AAA has been extremely helpful in providing information, statistics, and resources for community planning and organizing.

Societal Level

The OAA of 1965 created a significant national plan outlining goals and objectives for older adults. The objectives included adequate income; the best possible physical and mental health; suitable housing; full restorative services; the opportunity for employment; health in retirement; honor and dignity; civic, cultural, and recreational opportunities; efficient community services; benefits from research; and the ability to exercise individual initiatives in managing one's life (Hancock, 1990, pp. 233-234).

These objectives guide the Administration on Aging as it coordinates programs among government agencies that affect senior citizens. The refuge center program would promote mental health, bringing a sense of value and dignity, as well as recreational and civic opportunities, for older adults. Because the program entails the cooperation of an additional government agency, the park system, Carla will also contact the Administration on Aging to seek their advice and assistance.

Interestingly, both PPP members at Timberland and park officials expressed an interest in exploring the benefits of hiring employees versus those of utilizing volunteers. Clearly, low-income elderly would benefit if they were paid for duties performed at the animal refuge center. Carla is aware that the Senior Community Service Employment Program (Title V), authorized under the OAA, was created to encourage part-time employment of low-income seniors to enhance the general welfare of a community (Hancock, 1990, pp. 245-246). She will inquire into the status and appropriateness of any Title V or other grant monies for the proposed program at the animal refuge center.

Finally, Carla is committed to promoting the highest degree of respect for older adults who volunteer. She knows that not all volunteer experiences are positive. Thus, an explicit part of any agreement with the park system for volunteers from Timberland Senior Citizens Center will be AARP's Bill of Rights. A major component in Carla's social work practice with aging persons involves empowering older adults and enhancing their societal image as competent citizens.

International Level

Timberland Senior Citizens Center is located approximately 120 miles south of Canada. Therefore, the community is affected both socially and economically by its neighbor to the north. For example, there is direct international competition in both the timber and tourism industries. Nearly 20 percent of the visitors to the county park come from Canada. Since some of the Canadian visitors speak French, it is helpful that several senior citizens from Timberland are able to converse both in English and French.

Because seniors at Timberland readily receive Canadian news, many compare their Medicaid and Medicare benefits to those in Canada. This has led to lively discussions contrasting the quality of health care services in the two countries, the meaning of managed health care, and the consequences of increases in Medicare premiums for the elderly in the United States. Clearly, the spiralling cost of medical care for older adults is a major concern for Carla's clients.

Her close proximity to another country motivates Carla to develop a keen interest in international social work. In addition to keeping abreast of changes occurring in Canada that could affect her work directly (e.g., the possible secession of Quebec), Carla has read with interest publications concerned with the role of gerontological social work in other countries. She has found this knowledge valuable in reflecting upon her own practice, especially as it relates to macro practice.

Hang-Sau and Chi (1994, p. 80), working with the elderly in Hong Kong, submit that helping professionals often demonstrate a tendency to stress the role of teacher while disregarding the role of advocacy. They suggest that social workers, overburdened by the daily routine of working with older adults in senior citizen centers, often fail to focus on the significance of advocacy and the need to organize "concern groups."

In her work with the PPP, Carla has tended to use the meetings with the seniors as information-sharing sessions and has not adequately stressed the need for advocacy for their issues. In an effort to be neutral, she has felt reluctant to enter political forums and explore controversial issues with senior citizens. Hang-Sau and Chi's (1994) article has persuaded Carla to reevaluate her role at Timberland and to become more vocal in the discussion of political issues as well as to help the senior members exercise more direct political power.

APPLYING A SOCIAL WORK FRAMEWORK: SOCIAL RECONSTRUCTION THEORY

Chapter 8 began with an overview of social reconstruction theory. Old age as defined by society causes the elderly to feel incompetent and deficient. These feelings occur in part as a result of role loss when seniors are not encouraged to use their talents and skills after retirement. A sense of inadequacy and a decrease in self-esteem are frequently felt by older adults. This results in a loss to society of valuable experience and wisdom. Social reconstruction theory suggests themes of empowerment, self-rule, social power, and maintenance of integrity that social workers with older-age clients will want to integrate into their practice.

In our example, Carla addresses the needs and desires of senior citizens, but she places a special emphasis on seeking ways to advance their power and position in the community and society. Timberland seniors worry about their medical benefits, park system, and isolation from other members of society. They are also concerned about being "second-class citizens" whose opinions are seldom considered and whose voices are silenced. Decisions seem to be made about them and for them, seldom by them.

At the same request of her clients and agency, Carla entered the political arena to explore ways to advocate for the rights of senior citizens. Her involvement with Timberland's PPP, the AAA, the Administration on Aging, and the AARP enables her to gain valuable information for securing resources and empowering her clientele to reach their goals. Carla's willingness to become involved, to make influential contacts, and to enter political discourse has fostered a spirit of collective participation and action with the PPP and with Timberland.

Using social reconstruction theory allows Carla to look beyond micro-system levels. Older adults at Timberland want to contribute to their communities and society with the enthusiasm of a Jimmy Carter. However, their gifts go beyond either helping to establish peace in Haiti or achieving solvency for the animal refuge center and petting zoo. Their accumulated wisdom, available hours, mental energy, and desire to be included in decisions that affect lives are priceless gifts that mutually benefit seniors and the community. Carla has come to appreciate the desire of senior citizens to take their rightful, contributory, and respected place in society.

SUGGESTED ACTIVITIES

1. Ask a grandparent or other senior citizen for an opinion of America's view of aging. Does his or her perception coincide with elements of social reconstruction theory?

2. Does your university or social work program maintain formal linkage with senior citizen groups? What benefits could older adults bring to your college or department? With three other class members, explore your perceptions of the advantages and disadvantages of "being old in America."

3. Invite a representative of a senior citizens organization to speak to your class or school. Become familiar with the various ways that this organization promotes a positive image of older adults. List advocacy programs for the elderly that exist in your community.

4. Identify three or more major advancements in health, social services, and quality of life for older Americans since the Social Security Act of 1935.

226

REFERENCES

American Association of Retired Persons (1985). *To Serve—Not to Be Served: A Guide for Older Volunteers*. Washington, DC: American Association of Retired Persons.

Blackburn, J., & Chilman, C. (1987). The Probable Impact of Proposed Legislative and Budgetary Changes on the Lives of the Elderly and Their Families. *Journal of Gerontological Social Work*, 11(3/4), 19-42.

Carter, J. (1995). *Always a Reckoning*. New York: Times Books.

Carter, J., & Carter, R. (1987). *Everything to Gain: Making the Most of the Rest of Your Life*. New York: Random House.

Chambre, S. (1984). Is Volunteering a Substitute for Role Loss in Old Age? An Empirical Test of Activity Theory. *The Gerontologist*, 24(3), 292-298.

Cox, E., & Parsons, R. (1994). *Empowerment-Oriented Social Work Practice with the Elderly*. Pacific Grove, CA: Brooks/Cole Publishing Company.

Cox, H. (1993). *Later Life: The Realities of Aging*. Englewood Cliffs, NJ: Prentice-Hall, Inc.

Dade, L. (1994). *Elderhosteling USA!: An Elderhostel How-to Guide*. Ferndale, CA: Eldertime Publishing Company.

Day, C. (1993). The Organized Elderly: Perilous, Powerless, or Progressive? *The Gerontologist*, 33(3), 426-427.

The Economist (1989). Paying for Granny. 311(7605), 19-20.

Fischer, L., & Schaffer, K. (1993). *Older Volunteers: A Guide to Research and Practice*. Newbury Park, CA: Sage Publications.

Gallagher, S. (1994). Doing Their Share: Comparing Patterns of Help Given by Older and Younger Adults. *Journal of Marriage and the Family*, 56, 567-578.

Gist, J. (1992). Did Tax Reform Hurt the Elderly? *The Gerontologist*, 32(4), 472-477.

Goodman, C. (1984). Helper Bank: A Reciprocal Services Program for Older Adults. *Social Work*, 29(4), 397-398.

Hancock, B. (1990). *Social Work with Older People*. Englewood Cliffs, NJ: Prentice-Hall.

Hang-Sau, N., & Chi, I. (1994). Political Attitudes and Behaviors of the Elderly in Hong Kong: Implications for Social Work Practice. *Journal of Gerontological Social Work*, 21 (3/4), 71-82.

Harrigan, M., & Farmer, R. (1992). The Myths and Facts of Aging. In R. Schneider & N. Kript (Eds.), *Gerontological Social Work*. Chicago: Nelson-Hall.

Hoffman, S. (1983). Peer Counselor Training with the Elderly. *The Gerontologist*, 23(4), 358-360.

Jaynes, G. (1995). Eyes on the Prize. *Esquire*, October, 126-133.

Kuypers, J., & Bengtson, V. (1973). Social Breakdown and Competence. *Human Development*, 16, 181-201.

McKenzie, R. (1993). Senior Status: Has the Power of the Elderly Peaked? *The American Enterprise*, 4(1), 74-80.

Meyer, D., & Bartolomei-Hill, S. (1994). The Adequacy of Supplemental Security Income Benefits for Aged Individuals and Couples. *The Gerontologist*, 34(2), 161-172.

Modern Maturity (1995). Halting the Decline. November-December, pp. 12-14.

Morris, R., & Bass, S. (1986). The Elderly as Surplus People: Is There a Role for Higher Education? *The Gerontologist*, 26(1), 12-18.

Morrow-Howell, N., Lott, L., & Ozawa, M. (1990). The Impact of Race on Volunteer Helping Relationships among the Elderly. *Social Work*, 35(5), 395-402.

National Association of Social Workers (1990). *Code of Ethics*. Washington, DC: National Association of Social Workers.

Pena, X. (1996). M.S.U. Instructor Left Out in Cold. *Lansing State Journal*, August 14, 1B.

Perkins, K., & Tice, C. (1995). A Strengths Perspective in Practice: Older People and Mental Health Challenges. *Journal of Gerontological Social Work*, 23(3/4), 83-97.

Quadagno, J. (1991). Interest-Group Politics and the Future of U.S. Social Security. In J. Myles & J. Quadagno (Eds.), *States, Labor Markets, and the Future of Old-Age Policy*. Philadelphia: Temple University Press.

Rice, F. (1995). *Human Development: A Life-Span Approach.* Upper Saddle River, NJ: Prentice-Hall.

Shannon, B., Smiciklas-Wright, H., Davis, B., & Lewis, C. (1983). A Peer Educator Approach to Nutrition for the Elderly. *The Gerontologist*, 23(2), 123–126.

Staples, L. (1990). Powerful Ideas about Empowerment. *Administration in Social Work*, 14(2), 29–42.

Storey, J. (1986). Policy Changes Affecting Older Americans During the First Reagan Administration. *The Gerontologist*, 26(1), 27–31.

9

Achieving Social Justice and Empowerment

C hange is the essence of social work practice. Even though the problems of many clients are influenced by large-scale social ills, social workers may perceive them only at individual and family levels. To assess personal problems without ample consideration of social conditions is incomplete and inadequate. An individual assessment does not embrace social work's broader vision of human life and the fullness of human interaction. To achieve social justice and empower our clients, we must understand and find new ways to interact with the larger environment.

SOCIAL JUSTICE

Social workers have an obligation to promote social justice. Social work practice is grounded in the ethical principle that every person should have equitable access to needed

resources—for example, food, housing, jobs, and education. Social workers must evaluate control over resource allocation, the equitable distribution of resources, and whether resources are seen as "rights" or "privileges" (Reid and Billups, 1986). According to new accreditation standards of the Council on Social Work Education (CSWE), social work students need to understand the dynamics and consequences of social and economic injustice. The CSWE now mandates content that examines various forms and mechanisms of oppression and discrimination. In this final chapter we review how macro practice relates to various forms of social injustice.

Chapter 1 described the plight of a homeless Appalachian woman with children, focusing on the vulnerability of families in our society. Chapter 2 related economics, unemployment, and politics to the care and nurturing of infants. Clara Sherman's awareness of social change and its impact on the mothers and infants she serves elevates the issues to a macro level. Chapter 3 accentuated the impact of racism upon preschool children, and the need for parent education. In Chapter 4, as Melissa Richardson advocated for funds as well as for understanding of the needs of ADD children in the community, she accomplished goals on many levels. If her contact had been only an individual, therapeutic relationship with a few children, her work would have had a limited effect. Reviewing aspects of adolescence, in Chapter 5, we examined persecution that occurs as a result of social labels. Chapter 6 on young adulthood considered marital status, parenting issues, and sexual orientation, as well as discrimination against gays and lesbians. Gender discrimination in the labor force and role enactment were highlighted in discussing middle age, in Chapter 7. Enhancing the position of elderly Americans was the focus of Chapter 8. Combating ageism and the stigma of old age was emphasized as a macro responsibility for the social worker at Timberland Senior Citizens Center.

In the case examples, the assumption was that clients could pay for social work intervention or that service was provided under public or subsidized private auspices. Assessment, therefore, was **client driven**. Primary consideration was given to the needs of clients, not to their ability to pay for intervention.

In social work practice, however, clients often are unable to pay for services or are placed on agency waiting lists until resources become available. In such a **resource driven** system, clients often become impoverished while waiting for help. Assessment is frequently limited by what is realistically available through short-term intervention (Netting, Kettner, and McMurtry, 1993).

When analyzing macro-level systems, social workers should not ignore the nature of their own delivery system. Justice-related issues are enmeshed in the very workplace of social workers. Therefore agency practitioners should be alert when resources rather than client needs determine who receives service.

THE TIME CRUNCH

Macro-level assessment and subsequent intervention is an integral function of generalist social work practice. Yet, given the various resource and time constraints placed on social workers, how feasible is it for workers to engage in the kind of macro-level activities described in this book? As waiting lists in social work agencies increase, emergency concerns of clients tend to take precedence over macro-level considerations (Long, 1995).

Recognizing that social workers have excessive demands placed upon them, Brody and Nair (1995, p. 110) advise deliberate and formal planning concerning the use of the professional self, to determine priorities for the use of time. Specifically, as related to macro-level social work activities, Brody and Nair suggest the following scheme for priorities:

Priority	*Explanation*
Highest Priority	An activity that is both important and urgent because it provides the best payoff in accomplishing the organization's mission.
Medium Priority	Important, though not urgent. It is necessary to achieve a significant objective.
Low Priority	An activity that contributes only marginally to the achievement of an important objective.
Posteriority	Neither important nor urgent. It could be delayed, minimized, delegated, or even eliminated. (1995, p. 110)

This model is useful, particularly on an individual basis, for prioritizing macro-level activities. However, it fails to address the broader problem of securing adequate time for social workers to accomplish macro-level social work assessment and intervention strategies. Long (1995) suggests that collective political pressure from professional groups, including the National Association of Social Workers (NASW) and various voluntary associations, is crucial to demand that agencies define the role of social worker to include macro-level activities.

What is to be gained by promoting macro-level assessment and change if social workers have little or no time to give to these strategies? As a profession, social work must continue to assess ways to advance macro practice throughout the social service delivery system.

THE DIRECT/INDIRECT DISTINCTION

Traditionally, social work has been conceptualized into direct and indirect practice. **Direct practice** is primarily face-to-face contact with the client and focused on changing the client system, whether an individual, family, or small group. Conversely, **indirect practice** is distinguished as "less contact with a client system on a face-to-face basis...managing and developing programs, services, and policies that deal with social structures and resources" (Pierce, 1989, p. 157).

Social workers must question the value of maintaining this differentiation, however, particularly for macro social work endeavors. Using the direct/indirect distinction, the presentation of assessment in this book would be viewed as indirect practice. In terms of the importance of social work responsibilities, the term "indirect" connotes secondary or ancillary activities. However, we contend that developing and managing programs and policies that match resources and need is a primary function of social work.

Assessment in each chapter of this book was directed by a different sociological theory. By using theories of social disorganization, role, normalization, labeling, value-conflict, or social reconstruction orientation, social structure was stressed over the individual and family.

Case examples focused on macro social work functions. In the first chapter, social workers were encouraged to consider current trends toward managed care and interdisciplinary intervention. In his work with adolescents, Samuel's duties as a social worker at the Santa Louisa Community Center involved more than face-to-face interaction with teenagers. Samuel met regularly with community leaders, employers, and court officials on behalf of his clients. Carla, the social worker at Timberland Senior Citizens Center, challenged herself to become more politically involved and to develop contacts with local, state, and federal officials interested in championing senior causes. Should these be tagged as indirect social work methods? We conclude that macro-oriented activities are what distinguish social workers from other helping professionals.

The direct/indirect dichotomy places the social worker in an awkward position. Does performing of macro-level roles conflict with agency policy? Is the worker encouraged to utilize macro approaches or must she or he take the initiative in developing such intervention? Will Keith, the group social worker in a rural community action agency, continue to feel secure about his job if he participates in a multi-agency cluster group? What will be the agency response if he becomes actively involved in recreational and day care programs that benefit his clients?

At the least, social workers need to assess macro-level systems and become familiar with community and societal resources so that they may be effective brokers of services. Unfortunately, active involvement in macro practice activities is frequently disapproved by administrators concerned about large caseloads and reimbursement regulations that narrowly define billable services. This falls under the general rubric of what Meyer (1993, pp. 6–7) calls **pressures to think narrowly**, where

> it is felt that if one cannot resolve these major social problems, nor even grasp the complexity and fluidity of the social scene, the best recourse is to address the least complex, narrowest, most "doable," private or internal aspects of cases so as to demonstrate effectiveness and relieve continuing frustration.

ECOLOGICAL THEORY

Ecological theory emphasizes a complete ecosystems assessment. Different ecology-based paradigms have been presented depicting essential data collection in cases (Meyer, 1993, pp. 114-124). Most versions include culture, physical status, social environment (home, community, school, and work), person (cognitive, emotional, and behavioral aspects), significant others, as well as historic norms.

Explicit in most social work models for problem solving or planned change is a call for assessment and intervention with macro-level systems. "Practice situations often require practitioners to assess the factors present in a given situation and to relate them to a broad range of behaviors; behaviors potentially associated with more than one model of macro human service work" (Meenaghan, Washington, and Ryan, 1982, pp. 14-15). These authors suggest that social workers should possess technical competencies, relevant across models, that include "assessing and working with communities, complex organizations, and power configurations." Involvement in political action groups, persuasion of influential individuals to take action on urgent social problems, and promotion of new legislation are macro-level methods for addressing social injustices.

Students entering field instruction must carefully examine each agency's tool for assessing clients, traditionally called the social history. This instrument is an indicator of the field agency's orientation. How comprehensive is the assessment piece in the agency's treatment planning and documentation? Is it rooted in ecological theory or in some other theoretical orientation? Are macro-level elements and components, including an emphasis on social empowerment, specifically included? The student should be prepared to initiate dialogue relative to case issues with supervisors. Such discussion often leads to openness regarding macro approaches. On the other hand, students who are aware of deep investments in current policies and procedures should expect some resistance and should exercise diplomacy in developing social work skills.

THE STRENGTHS PERSPECTIVE

Recent social work publications highlight the **strengths perspective**, a creative reaction to the obsession with problems, pathologies, and deficits. Practice is centered on "eliciting and articulating clients' internal and external resources" (Saleebey, 1992, p. 3).

By focusing on client strengths, this perspective shifts assessment away from an individualistic, problem-based approach to "ecological (social, political, and cultural, as well as individual) accounts of human predicaments and possibilities" (Saleebey, 1992, p. 4). Using the strengths perspective, social workers focus on identifying previously unrecognized individual and/or group resources, and are less inclined to define clients only in terms of ego deficiencies, behavioral problems, or family dysfunctions. Social workers are challenged to discover the power and resourcefulness within people (individually and collectively) while avoiding the mind-set of blaming the victim (Ryan, 1976).

Saleebey describes the strengths perspective in relationship to social work assessment:

> Recognizing client strengths is fundamental to the value stance of the profession. It provides for a leveling of the power social workers have over clients and in so doing presents increased potential for the facilitation of a partnership in the working relationship. Focusing on strengths in assessment has the potential for liberating clients from stigmatizing diagnostic classifications that reinforce "sickness" in family and community environments. (1992, pp. 140–141)

Clearly, assessment from a strengths perspective places a primary emphasis on both environmental and individual strengths. Macro-level assessments of organizations, communities, societies, and countries identify, clarify, and articulate resources and possibilities for planned change. As with other forms of assessment, this dynamic process involves a partnership between client and social worker.

Empowerment is a key concept in the strengths perspective. "Empowerment usually means to return a voice to silenced or disenfranchised people" (Tice and Perkins, 1996, p. 9). Beyond the identification of social ills, empowerment entails discovering the power within individuals, families, groups, and neighborhoods. By focusing on resources and power, the strengths perspective fosters energy and vision for developing social policies and programs that enable clients to gain significant control over their lives.

To illustrate this point, we were tempted to concentrate on current, difficult issues facing many middle-aged women. While serious and distressing problems for women occur during middle age, we made a conscious effort to emphasize the positive aspects and benefits of this life segment for females. For many women, midlife is also a time of liberation, providing distinct advantages. One must move beyond perspectives of midlife women that are based on sexism and gender-role stereotypes (Hunter and Sundel, 1994, p. 113). By focusing on strengths and benefits of middle age, as opposed to deficits, social workers can better empower women to seek positive means to enrich their lives.

As we considered older age, a major emphasis was placed on social empowerment. Individual and collective options to influence program and policy development were principal themes. The Pulse and Power Program at Timberland Senior Citizens Center exemplified how client strengths could be directed into active involvement in important community and national issues. The Center program encouraged older adults to exercise their collective influence.

Our goal has been to integrate a strengths perspective. We have been eclectic in approaching theoretical perspectives, and we encourage the reader to consider a variety of approaches in assessing the social environment.

When engaged in social work practice, you will find some helping professionals who rely solely on one theoretical orientation and who assess every client within this framework. Do these professionals have superior clinical skills and insight or do they need to embrace a broader selection of theories? Might such single-focus persons have simply chosen to avoid the complexities of macro analyses?

VALUES AND CONTROLLING BIAS

Social workers, like other practitioners, are subject to biases. Each social worker approaches assessment with a distinct background and set of experiences. Her or his own cultural, political, ethnic, generational, psychological, educational, and gender orientation will influence how the client's problems are viewed. The challenge for social workers is to be objective when entering into partnerships with clients (Meyer, 1993). Assessment in social work should be client-centered. When social workers gravitate toward micro-level analysis as a result of their education and training, macro assessment is often compromised. To offset this inclination, case examples in this book deemphasize micro-level in favor of macro-level systems.

Beyond the effects of educational and theoretical influences, an **organization's culture** influences how social workers think and behave (Brody and Nair, 1995, p. 17). The culture of one's place of employment not only establishes formal goals, but also communicates an informal sense of the correct way of doing things in that setting. Organizational values therefore may constitute a potent source of bias.

Recall that Melissa Richardson, a school social worker, found the Hogan City School System to be receptive and supportive of her activities with a collaborative attention deficit disorder group (ATTEND). The school's organizational culture allowed Melissa to consult with school staff and parents in considering program and policy changes that would benefit children with attention deficit disorders. However, if Melissa had been working in a less progressive school system, the organizational culture could have been far less accepting of her macro-level assessment and intervention endeavors. Faculty and school officials often are territorial and protective with regard to teaching practices. In a more restrictive climate, Melissa's efforts to introduce policy changes could have been interpreted as interference in the work of teachers and school officials and construed by them as unprofessional behavior.

Organizational culture and values affect how social workers view assessment. These factors can encourage or discourage social workers from thinking about the "big picture" for clients.

The graduate considering a social work position should be aware of the organizational climate. Is there a primary concern for the client as a consumer? Is there a sense of trust, emotional bonding, and pride in one's work among workers at the agency? Do social workers at the agency embrace a single theoretical orientation or are they eclectic? Are employees committed to macro social work practice?

ENTERTAINING AN INTERNATIONAL PERSPECTIVE

Advances in technology, communication, and transportation serve to connect communities, states, and countries in ways never before imagined. The profound effects associated with advancements in technology and an emerging global economy have compelled social workers to be increasingly international in approaching practice.

For decades, social workers have acknowledged that a broader, more global understanding of the social environment is needed in the social work profession (Friedlander, 1975). Social work, for example, has a rich tradition in various international relief efforts. This has included significant involvement in the International Red Cross, the Peace Corps, and the United Nations Relief and Rehabilitation Administration. Social workers have also actively worked to improve world health conditions and championed international efforts to alleviate the impoverishment of children and families (for example, the United Nations Children's Fund—UNICEF).

Beyond humanitarian efforts to help victims in other countries, social workers now find that a global view is often necessary for accurate and effective assessment and intervention in the lives of their clients. Whether through cultural sensitivity, economic interdependence, or consideration of foreign policies, the social work profession continues to affirm the importance of an international perspective in problem solving and planned change.

Each chapter of this book contains a section devoted to considering relevant international issues in relationship to case examples. In Chapter 6, David's presenting problem during young adulthood is directly related to his desire to emigrate from Jamaica to the United States. **International social work**

> should focus on the profession and practice in different parts of the world, especially the place of the organized profession in different countries, the different roles that social workers perform, the practice methods they use, the problems they deal with, and the many challenges they face. (Hokenstad, Khinduka, and Midgley, 1992, p. 4)

In contrast, **international social welfare**, sometimes referred to as comparative social policy, is defined as the analysis of socioeconomic policies and human services in different countries. In this book we have utilized both concepts.

As a result of her study of social work practice in China, Carla Peters (Chapter 8) was motivated to reevaluate her role as a social worker with older adults at Timberland Senior Citizens Center. She decided to give greater attention to advocacy while continuing to share information regarding issues that affect older adults. She utilizes insights from international social work practice as she assumes an advocacy role.

In Chapter 4, Melissa Richardson used the Internet to "surf the web" and examine policies, research, and the delivery of services to children with attention deficit disorders in other countries. One of her goals was to compare other programs and policies with those of the United States. Her use of these resources confirms the value of international social welfare.

Social workers, however, need not be directly involved with international social work or international social welfare to gain from knowledge of other countries. Because social work is a profession that is sensitive to contemporary issues, assessment should reflect current conditions in the environment. A careful examination of local, national, and international events must be included in the evaluation of each case.

MACRO-LEVEL ASSESSMENT AND THE FUTURE

Given the social, political, and economic climate of the times, social work needs to be understood as a function of prevention rather than remediation. How can social workers promote change in the social environment in order to prevent problems rather than focusing on the rehabilitation of clients and their individual needs (Chetkow-Yanoov, 1992, p. 77)?

The case examples in this book reflect primarily **remedial service**. Social workers were called into action to deal with some specific difficulty (Garvin and Tropman, 1992, p. 182). At a macro level, the concern was for identifying systemic elements causing the problem(s).

The social work profession is challenged to focus on macro-social conditions and to identify various populations at risk. This constitutes **preventive targeting**, which can reduce the incidence of a particular problem (Bloom, 1981, p. 15).

You will remember that, in Chapter 2, Clara Sherman headed the Infants' Milk Fund and Prenatal Clinic. Following a community needs assessment, women with severe mental illness and their infants were identified as populations at risk. Clara's efforts were clearly directed at improving social conditions through employment and day care to ensure proper growth and nurturing of infants. Preventive targeting enabled the worker to promote health and well-being among a high-risk population in her community.

In Chapter 4 on normalization and children of school age, major attention was given to identifying schools and students at risk. The intent was to challenge the reader to consider strategies for improving educational programs and services including curriculum, technology, and economic decisions benefiting school children at risk of academic failure. Preventive targeting encouraged assessment of educational alternatives.

The importance of preventive targeting in the assessment component of social work practice cannot be overemphasized.

> We will never be able to solve collective problems by treating its victims one by one. We should have some helping professionals look at the sources of these problems in an effort to proact, to reduce environmental stresses and to augment the strengths in populations of persons at risk or with potential, rather than having always to react after the fact to persons made miserable by problems and illness. (Bloom, 1981, p. 213)

Finally, as social work educators, we encourage social work students and practitioners to develop creative imaginations. The challenging new frontiers continue to expand our opportunities to interact with the diverse skills, data, and practices of social workers around the world.

Technology makes macro contacts possible as we share new insights and information with those who seek our partnerships in achieving their greatest potential. Social workers committed to that goal will thrive on the broad horizons opening to us. As macro social work practice develops, it promises major dividends for clients and society.

REFERENCES

Bloom, M. (1981). *Primary Prevention: The Possible Science.* Englewood Cliffs, NJ: Prentice-Hall.

Brody, R., & Nair, M. (1995). *Macro Practice: A Generalist Approach.* Wheaton, IL: Gregory Publishing Company.

Chetkow-Yanoov, B. (1992). *Social Work Practice: A Systems Approach.* New York: The Haworth Press.

Friedlander, W. (1975). *International Social Welfare.* Englewood Cliffs, NJ: Prentice-Hall.

Garvin, C., & Tropman, J. (1992). *Social Work in Contemporary Society.* Englewood Cliffs, NJ: Prentice-Hall.

Hokenstad, M., Khinduka, S., & Midgley, J. (1992). *Profiles in International Social Work.* Washington, DC: NASW Press.

Hunter, S., & Sundel, M. (1994). Midlife for Women: A New Perspective, *Affilia*, 9(2), 113-128.

Long, D. (1995). Attention Deficit Disorder and Case Management: Infusing Macro Social Work Practice. *Journal of Sociology and Social Welfare*, 12(2), 45-50.

Meenaghan, T., Washington, R., & Ryan, R. (1982). *Macro Practice in the Human Services.* New York: The Free Press.

Meyer, C. (1993). *Assessment in Social Work Practice.* New York: Columbia University Press.

Netting, E., Kettner, P., & McMurtry, S. (1993). *Social Work Macro Practice.* White Plains, NY: Longman.

Pierce, D. (1989). *Social Work and Society: An Introduction.* White Plains, NY: Longman.

Reid, P., & Billups, J. (1986). Distributional Ethics and Social Work Education. *Journal of Social Work Education*, 22(1), 6-17.

Ryan, W. (1976). *Blaming the Victim* (revised). New York: Vintage Books.

Saleebey, D. (1992). *The Strengths Perspective in Social Work Practice.* White Plains, NY: Longman.

Tice, C., & Perkins, K. (1996). *Mental Health Issues and Aging.* Pacific Grove, CA: Brooks/Cole Publishing Company.

Index

MACRO SYSTEMS IN THE SOCIAL ENVIRONMENT
Edited by John Beasley
Production supervision by Kim Vander Steen
Cover design by Lesiak/Crampton Design, Inc., Park Ridge, Illinois
Composition by Point West, Inc., Carol Stream, Illinois
Paper, Finch Opaque
Printed and bound by Quebecor Printing, Fairfield, Pennsylvania